# The Cheesecake Theory of Crime

# The Cheesecake Theory of Crime

## An Irreverent View of Justice in America

DANIEL S CAMPAGNA PH.D.

**The Cheesecake Theory of Crime**

ISBN: 151700067X
ISBN 13: 9781517000677
Library of Congress Control Number: 2015914262
CreateSpace Independent Publishing Platform
North Charleston, South Carolina

Dedication

To Kaela, Kai, Braelyn and Noa

# Table of Contents

# One

## The Ice Cream Truck and Justice

*"Americans, like human beings everywhere,
believe many things that are obviously
untrue. Their most destructive untruth
is that it is very easy for any American to
make money. They will not acknowledge
how in fact hard money is to come by, and,
therefore, those who have no money blame and
blame and blame themselves. This inward
blame has been a treasure for the rich and
powerful, who have had to do less for their
poor, publicly and privately, than any other
ruling class since, say Napoleonic times."*

Kurt Vonnegut, Slaughterhouse-Five

**"B**efore the facts" (Pro Res) get started allow me to set the tone and context for this irreverent treatise on crime and justice in America. This is a casual conversation about the nature of crime, criminals, and the systems and laws used to dole out justice. Also, there is ample Latin phrasing to familiarize you with terms and ideas commonly used in criminal justice. I am, however, writing this for the layperson. Practitioners, academicians, buzzard politicians and sundry other camp groupies can shake their heads and wonder why the nurse has not rolled the medication trolley over to me. A few blue and red ones would be swell. They might add some focus to knotty problems about justice.

Problems such as happy ever after in the courts of law and just deserts; that bad guys get caught and things always work out in the end. It is far better for us to cling to our myths about justice and heroes like my Uncle Phil who drove an ice cream and was fond of saying – "Those goddamn illegals will steal me blind". And he was right. Uncle Phil went blind but it was old man diabetes and glaucoma that narrowed his vision to that of a pinhole in black cardboard. But we believed in Uncle Phil's myth of a kindly man who sold ice cream to children chasing after his truck. That's how myths get started. He seemed to be doing the right thing. Personally the glaucoma version was more interesting to me as a kid. That goddamn truck smelled like spoiled fruit and corduroy farts…. and to hell with Uncle Phil. Come to think of it he never gave me a freebie. Ever.

So it is with crime and justice in the empire of America. No freebies and way too many myths. This book will explain in broad brush strokes "how some things are" in the worlds of adult and juvenile justice. After 30 years of working in these systems, becoming a Ph.D. (please, hold back your applause), doing grunt level field research in the gut ugly world of sexual trafficking in children, of investigating and interviewing many picturesque characters of crime and their victims, visiting prisons, jails and "insane asylums" in various states, working as a poorly trained deputy sheriff/ correctional officer, state investigator, and certified dispute mediator, among other things, I am going to bare all and heave my knowledge back over the fence. Let me not forget to confess to being a hard core juvenile delinquent with specialties in weapons and explosives and property damage with a side order of assaults. A right anarchist prick you could say, angry at everything.

To help with this narrative, I have selected a small group of issues and conundrums of sustained interest to me. Disagree all you want with my conclusions; I am often wrong, irrational and temperamental. The examples and vignettes, the frustration and anger housed within these pages, however, is authentic, to the bone. It seems that this nation of the semi-united states (here's looking at you Texas and South Carolina!) has devolved into an oligarchy-corporate state. Worse, the media controls the agenda about justice. Too many people respond to blogs and comments online with ignorant, spiteful remarks that prevent honest discourse. This is especially true in the arenas of crime, justice, violence, and the related issues of race and poverty. The advent of global discussion in the forms of anonymous comments (please abolish anonymity and make all commenters identify themselves with full name and contact information!) encourages the dark side of human personalities. Social media sites and blogging options offer more channels for dispersing hateful commentary. Coupled with a visually based learning society (if you cannot take a photo of "it" why bother with the experience?"), we have opened a giant spillway of vitriol, gross deformities of thought, and a collective hunger for narcissism ("Let me take a selfie in front of that car crash.").

But that is me spouting from the pulpit. Those broadcast mediums enable and empower people who are anathema to the broader ideas of kindness, love, and understanding of alternative views. Every minute of every day these digital formats provide ready access to the pulpit preachers and trolls of the Interweb (my term). The most despicable behaviors are condoned or framed provocatively so that any mistake by the author is overlooked in the interests of sensationalism. Or else the agitator tries to cover up his/her tracks with lies e.g. birthers, creationists, conspiracy fans. Otherwise, every human condition is fair game for ridicule and threats that should qualify for official investigation or arrest are either ignored or overlooked. There are, simply put, no practical consequences for the anonymous zealot, with precious few exceptions. A person's skin color, appearance, gender, religion or status as a victim can be challenged and distorted. This is described as a form of free speech, even though the courts have repeatedly noted that free speech is not without its limits. Justice, therefore, is certainly an adjustable term depending on context. It becomes a very emotional, often racially or sexually biased concept, in which the speaker's fears and hatreds are applied to others. Ignorance, loathing, and discrimination are not supposed to be a part of the bailiwick of justice (or the criminal justice systems) but clearly they are specters in the courts of public opinion. Try a sample or two from the "Candy Box of Unfettered Free Speech":

## Sample 1
### (Re: graffiti on the confederate statute in Charleston, SC after the church shootings)

CaptSapto said: "ALL LIVES MATTER"! That is what we should be striving for. When blacks stop causing so much crime, killing each other and blaming the establishment for all their misfortune and join the whole of the country in furthering the cause of liberty and justice, only then will "ALL LIVES MATTER"!

Translation: CaptSapto is saying that black people are the root of most crime. That is known as *blaming the victim(s)*. It is a common response in criminal justice and society as shown in the following examples:

- Women should not dress "provocatively". It encourages sexual assaults. Men can apparently dress however they wish.
- Be aware of one's surroundings. He/she was in the wrong place at the wrong time.

- They (victims) were "asking for it."
- Sometimes children need to be hit to teach them to behave. Behavior modification through the odd whack to the face or spanking.
- Tainted water supply because of chemical spills in the area? Sell your house dumbass and move.
- You live in a poor neighborhood; you better expect to get hurt. Sucks for you.
- The victim got what he/she deserved under the circumstances.
- You should not ever disobey a police officer or else you better expect to get arrested or shot.
- Victims' status: If black, brown, blue, plaid, gay, disabled, transgender, mentally retarded people, etc. would stop looking for entitlements, work harder, stop committing crimes, vote, then racism and hatred would evaporate. Snap! Just like that.

And what I consider to a classic response, one of complete indifference or disregard to the victim, oft used and abused – "*Better Him Than Me!*" The wonder of blaming the victim is its convenience and simplicity; attaching simplistic descriptors to complex behaviors or issues enables the speaker to avoid confronting other realities about crime while feeling very self-satisfied for having solved a problem (crime) that has eluded the brightest minds of civilization for a few thousand years.

## Sample 2
### (Re: a video incident of Chicago cop opening fire on a car full of unarmed black teens)

Erict responded:  "You don't start firing into a car full of unarmed people. You just don't do that. You sure do if they aren't ceasing and desisting. The cop had no way to judge their motives. This is gotcha journalism at its best."

Translation: Erict is saying that if a police officer orders you to "cease and desist" and you fail to obey, all bets are off and the officer can and should shoot you/us. Often. Except police are notoriously bad shots statistically speaking so bring extra ammo, officer, reload and let 10-20 rounds of high velocity lead fly randomly and far throughout a neighborhood? After all, according to popular opinion, one should never disobey a police officer under any circumstances. The closing remark is also sarcastic.

## Sample 3
### (Re: Mother beaten senseless in front of her children by a passenger aboard a cruise ship after an argument about noisy children in the halls. Nothing happened to the assailant. No charges were filed.)

Mcworld said: "Was there at any time a way to de-escalate the situation? Because the story makes it seem like you were verbally aggressive before said incident."

Translation: Verbally aggressive? That qualifies for a major league beat down with serious head injuries? It is the American way to resolve conflicts. I make no claims to be a Boy Scout on good behavior or blameless with my past. My exposure to violence has lasted a lifetime and will doubtless continue to do so until the big leap into infinity. But this simple argument aboard a cruise ship led to a very violent attack that caused a concussion, scarring and other physical injuries. All of which happened in front of the woman's children.

So, let's make a friendly wager. I bet you that when you are done reading this book it may make you uncomfortable (or itchy and I can recommend some multi-purpose hand cream) and perhaps, just maybe, some of those popular myths about our justice system will look tarnished and useless, such as -

*Justice is blind.*
*The innocent cannot be convicted.*
*We have never executed an innocent person.*
*Everyone is equal under the law.*
*Or, one of my favorites – if you do nothing wrong you have nothing to worry about from the police or the courts.*

That one always evokes a pleasant chuckle. It is an absurd idea that an adult can move through life without "doing something wrong". In any event, the single most urgent expectation of this short book is that readers might use critical thought rather than raw, dark emotions and piss ant killing stereotypes before opening their thoughts on the Interweb or in daily conversations. That's it.

Just consider alternative viewpoints without needing to "win" the argument or using violence to make one's point. This nation has been at war since the arrival of the first colonists, muskets in one hand and a bible in the other. The American response to social problems has traditionally been to declare a war. Notice the language. War = some level of aggression that excels in success. Except almost all of these social crusades / jihads have failed repeatedly and have periodically amplified the problem e.g. drugs, gangs. Officially proclaimed wars against the homeless, alcohol / drugs abuse, gangs, AIDS (we are winning that one but only because there is money to be made in selling the drugs), poverty, racism, terrorism, illegal immigrants, education, crime, and obesity fill our history books. I especially find that last war on "fatness" ironic. Ours is not a society that tolerates overweight, "abnormal" or unattractive people (elderly, disabled, too short, mentally retarded, etc.) with warmth or forbearance. It is typical of us, by way of reminder, to associate unattractive or disabled people with criminal activity ("Aha! I knew that wife beater was a mean looking twat!"). That is one of several reasons why we crave mugshot photos of the accused as though the images might reveal something about the monster within (even though the accused might later be acquitted). We are hoping to confirm our impressions of the offender by locking onto some physical trait. Being different can be its own crime, so to speak, if by different we mean accused of a crime. Once charged and placed onto the judicial conveyor belt, by the way, you are JWF (jolly well fucked) acquitted but more on that later in the book.

Speaking of appearance, do not look for a dry academic treatise in this book. I gave up on the papyrus approach to scholarly research. If my writing reads like a textbook, my apologies. That is not my goal. I want so speak clearly and honestly about the issues. Much of the research in Criminal Justice is notorious for using language so convoluted and tortured that only a handful of like-minded people and S&M fans will have the remotest chance of understanding. The working language of academia is often so intentionally dull and exclusive that it is the rough equivalent of mental masturbation. A warm, sticky feeling after drafting another tedious analysis of gang behavior in Philadelphia using bivariate regression and a literature review? Yum! Put that sweet little study on the bed while I pour some champagne and dim the lights.

This book is for merriment and dancing and rolling a jaybird after the kiddies are asleep. I also admit that I do not have an iota of compassion for the hateful, roller coaster public dialog about the value of life and its "easy come, easy go" status. No thanks. Not easy to admit in print but I despise those people who spew an endless stream of bitterness and bile while offering nothing constructive in return. To those tunnel visionaries, those one size fits all problems people ("Hey Uncle Phil!, Hey Rush L.!") I am sorry that your lives did not pan out as you hoped. Whose ever does but can't we dial down the hatred and bigotry a few decibels?

# The Cheesecake Theory of Crime

This guidebook, in other words, is of no use to "negative nabobs". Basic reforms, however, are provided as bricks in a very long, rocky path for further conversation. Keep in mind that many of the major historical reforms in criminal justice in America e.g. probation, hallway houses, foster care, etc. were introduced by civilians. Which means that the reader may either draw some inspiration from the proposed reforms or offer even better ideas for the adult and/or juvenile justice systems. Either way, the message is simple; one individual (you) can be the architect of change in criminal justice. This can be accomplished despite public and official resistance to constructive ideas for criminal justice. I wish to assure you of that point – you, the reader, can and must be the catalyst for change because the criminal justice system is not a self-correcting gyroscope.

> "Our problem is that people are obedient all over the world in the face of poverty and starvation and stupidity, and war, and cruelty. Our problem is that people are obedient while the jails are full of petty thieves… (And) the grand thieves are running the country. That's our problem."
>
> Howard Zinn

Zinn makes perfect sense. Being dutiful (submissive, quiet) little citizen-soldier-patriots allows for excess and abuse by government and its agents of justice. Bear in mind that those agents, some but not all, cheat defendants of their criminal rights, expose the façade of fairness, and continue to do so with little fear of oversight or repercussions. The concept of qualified immunity, for example, shields officials e.g. politicians, judges, police from litigation in the lawful performance of their official duties. I know about that concept having served a term as a Mayor of a small town in Missouri. I was cognizant of the fact that my personal assets in a lawsuit could be at risk depending on my behavior and decisions as a public official. Yet this very shield can muffle any and all effective reform efforts aimed at the accountability of government agents. Very few police officers, judges or prosecutors, for instance, are ever charged or convicted for official malfeasance.

This book, moreover, is going nowhere with readers who "know the truth". Their minds have long since slammed shut. The multi-tiered system of submerged, waterproofed, chambered, locked vaults at Fort Knox has nothing on those people who stopped learning, thinking and challenging (see blog samples above). However, I appreciate a thoughtful (evidence based, scientific method) argument rather than slipshod rebuttals. Make a convincing argument worth hearing. I am a pretty decent listener. As the reader has already detected, this is a "deposition" about crime and justice that is irreverent and audacious in its basic assumptions. As noted earlier, a number of phrases in Latin (pro se = before the facts) are included in the narrative because Latin is still the classical language of criminal justice in this country and using it will wow the folks at your next social event. Let's assume everyone has a need for using Latin in everyday life – "Mitha, quis vicis does nudist castra patefacio?" aka "Mitha, what time does the nudist camp open?" You know, the important stuff. And please leave your Speedos at home.

There is not much that is one dimensional about crime and justice in America. Much of the nuanced analysis found in academic reports is missing here. I offer precious little context to guide the reader. My own interpretation – <u>The Cheesecake Theory of Crime</u> – in Chapter 4 is a summary rather than a dissertation. That theory, with some fine tuning, has guided my thoughts on crime for years. This book is simply a collection of brief essays laden with 30 years of observations and involvement in the justice systems as a victim, offender, practitioner, and scholar. I have broken laws over the decades and pushed or exceeded the legal limits of many deviant acts. How I evaded being incarcerated is an example of life's lottery of consequences and I won. My perspectives are drawn from an eclectic set of credentials and experiences. An assortment of sources (Looking Elsewhere) is also included to help the reader find ready access to some of the more original, fact-based organizations and resources available within the domain of crime and justice and to help set the mood for further discourse. I encourage you to study these issues and sources further and decide for yourselves. The waters of contemplation, so to speak, are deep and I clearly have no stranglehold on the truth, whatever form it may assume. Find a reliable navigator and bring a compass. In that regard you are on your own but I am confident you will find something here to raise one's hackles. In the final section of this book are a few parting comments about rights, freedom, and the costs of doing justice in America.

A few closing words about my family history might also be in order. They tie into many of the underlying issues in this guidebook and help frame my overall perspective on justice. My great grandfathers came to America from Sicily and Rome (Campagna = countryside). Both entered the country at Ellis Island as immigrants whose names were quickly changed from beautiful names e.g. Salvatore Giuseppe Campagna to "Samuel" by the entry officials. Immigrants! Actually, isn't everyone in this country linked to an immigrant except for Native Americans? No matter. These two men worked in the Chicago area, one as a grocer and the other as a Republican alderman. The Sicilian grandfather never spoke anything, I was told, but Sicilian and pigeon English; his wife and kids translated for him. He had to cope with the neighborhood thugs common to Little Italy, manage a business, help raise a family, try to be a Catholic, and integrate into American society. Both men and millions of other citizens endured the nightmare of the Great Depression of the 1920"s, Prohibition, and political – corporate corruption on a scale that was unprecedented in its awfulness. Both served in the Army in WWI with the American Expeditionary Force. Both grandfathers died in their 50's, respectfully poor, survived by their wives, my loving grandmothers. My father served with the Signal Corps in WW2 in North Africa and France. He returned home to join the floodtide of young servicemen seeking the American Dream in the form of a suburban house, a steady job, a wife to raise the family, and two weeks of vacation. He was a union electrician and operated a security business on the side for extra income. All of my four uncles fought in WW2 in various theaters of war. Military service is a recurrent theme in my family spanning three generations. My brother James served (Army) and fought in the War of Vietnam. My family was marginal lower middle class; he and I did not have much as kids but we made it last.

Also, before letting go of this memory trip, it is worth noting that my father was a dead-eye shot with long range rifles (.30-.30 caliber) and trap shooting, winning stacks of trophies in the span of three decades. He and I joined the National Rifle Association (NRA) before it became a political mouthpiece and lobbying whore for the gun industry and right-wing haters ("Come on boyos, what exactly is the purpose of an assault rifle? Who do you intend to assault, eh?"). He recruited me to a rifle team, taught me about guns and their safety, how to properly clean weapons, reload ammunition, and a lasting respect for their finality of purpose. Guns have only three functions: to hunt (which I used to do), to compete in different shooting venues (which I did but not very well), and to kill. The latter function is absolute and irreversible, at least until we develop a Lazarus vaccine. Gun collections, by the way, are for show and tell, much in the same manner that one collects stamps, tropical parrots and obscure artwork from around the world.

All of which is to say that none of us are strangers to violence caused by crime. Violence arrives in many forms from guns to defective products to drunken assailants. How we respond to the chronic issues surrounding crime and justice says much about us and how far we have moved along the train tracks of ethical conduct. You know, ideas like respect for the rights of the accused. That being said, however, I do not accept or recognize this generation of left-wing, politically correct apologists e.g. "He killed his parents because they denied him a new cell phone but with time we can restore him to a "good place." Evidently you have no comprehension of victims' rights, inherently evil people (chronic offenders) or the pathology of criminal deviance. Stop apologizing for the offender, in other words, and concentrate on the victim.

Conversely, I do not understand, not even a teeny, weeny bit the notion that right-wing, white conservative, haters of anyone who offends or opposes the social order (flag, family, church), should be given the right to vote, to speak in public settings, even to reproduce. They preach a message of racial superiority not remotely grounded in scientific fact and disguise it as patriotism and universal justice. Except justice is not universally applied. The eugenics movement, the Tuskegee Syphilis Experiment, beating up Selma civil rights protestors, and other practices too numerous to list, are examples of people in power treating the powerless as lab rats. You right-wing folks applaud those activities because some lives matter a whole lot less than yours.

Neither a liberal or conservative philosophy defines this guidebook. The very good news is that the adult and juvenile criminal justice systems are really all-encompassing mirrors that reflect all that is honorable and horrific about us as a species. It is the same mirror used by the naked Emperor whose subjects lied about his choice of wardrobes. There is, consequently, very little that is halfway or cautious about my commentary. And barring blindness or blinders the mirror of criminal justice is utterly, totally unforgiving in its truthfulness. Some of us are, indeed, nasty buggers who have no other functions than to inhale air, occupy space and cause society small and big amounts of harm and destruction. We could do quite well without them.

Then there are the faithful citizens. My father, ex-vet, die-hard Republican, loyal taxpayer and citizen, racist, and fervent believer of the American Dream and social obedience, in his early 80's, was arrested for bumping his rubber trash can against a passing car. He was locked up in an interview room for five hours without access to his essential blood thinner medications (prior heart attacks and a stroke). The officers were notified of his health condition and they became belligerent and refused to give him access to the pills. He had to appear in court for his actions. Sorry pop, you deserved better from the system you supported all of your life.

I am also fairly certain that this is the last time I will ever write about any topic relating to crime and justice. I have written four other books, numerous articles, two plays, a state report, manuals, board games, and other publications in a variety of disciplines. Criminal Justice is a field ripe with opportunity for extolling virtue and shouting one's angst but enough is probably enough in my case. I have experienced an extremely eclectic life (by choice) that may prevent you from easily placing me in any descriptive category. During the course of that "career building" life it was my good fortune to meet some of the more marvelous human beings that our species could create as well as some of the more ruptured ducklings who committed acts so heinous and maleficent (evil) that it would have been better, in retrospect, had they never been born. I do not believe all life is sacred, by the way, and nowhere is this more evident to me than in the discipline of Criminal Justice. What I do argue fervently is that optimism is not a forlorn belief, that love is a more powerful emotion than hatred and contempt, and that we are being given an opportunity to restore the scales of justice with something more approximate to honesty, even handed-treatment, and a reminder that all levels of government (local, state, and federal) were originally designed to serve their citizens, and not the other way around.

And no, I have no ironclad solutions to the challenges posed by a ruptured criminal justice system. I do have an assortment of ideas worth discussing, adding to and subtracting from, and an open invitation for practical remedies. My concern is accountability. As a culture and a nation devoted to lofty but constantly violated principles of equality and freedom, I advocate for plain talk, less bullshit (meetings, circle jerk committees, federal grants to study much of nothing), and more field testing of ideas. Ideas like eliminating small cash bonds for indigent defendants in all jurisdictions. Like full funding and staffing for the office of public defenders.

# The Cheesecake Theory of Crime

Like external, non-governmental oversight of state and FBI crime labs (they have made so many errors in testing evidence as false positives), a massive overhaul of police officer standards and training (POST), and …but I get way ahead of myself. Let's try this a few wee steps at a time.

The Criminal Justice system (adult and juvenile) is a mix of good intentions, lofty goals, and humans who, by default of the species, function well sometimes and very poorly too often. How we administer our judicial systems and structure the future seems to hinge closely on our sense of fundamental fairness and an appreciation for irony and contradiction. Thomas Jefferson, for instance, a founding father of the American Constitution, declared equality was a natural condition of mankind. Thomas Jefferson owned and had sex with his female slaves; "Ladies, the mambo line to my bedroom forms at the door!" The American Constitution, not the Founding Fathers (slave and land owners) or Jefferson and his amorous appetite for African slaves and his odd notion of equality, forms the bedrock of the criminal justice system. So, perhaps the point of this book is that ethics and justice and equality are not mutually exclusive terms. Label me a hopeless eccentric but I do not consider the presence of the following behaviors to be a part of any healthy society:

- Legally carry an assault rifle into a public place such as an airport, library, and church.
- Fly a Confederate flag as a symbol and reminder to black citizens of racial scorn by whites.

- Declaring creationism to be a legitimate piece of a science curriculum because some God said so.
- Use Interweb sites as a platform for spreading commentary on how inferior other people or social classes are compared to white Christianity or Muslims or any religion that is intolerant of others. Come to think of it -take your pick. Most religions practice intolerance in some form.
- Exploit, beat, maim and kill children.
- Form militia and vigilante groups in the name of some extreme ideology.
- Eavesdrop on all digital transmissions without a court-issued warrant.

How are we improved by such behaviors? I must stop. That list would devour the rest of this book.

# Maxim

Possibly we could benefit from a dose of reality about justice that is not foisted upon us with threats of punishment and ostracism? Maybe there is still time and opportunity to change our headlong, angst driven rush into the chasm of civil disorder and unrest that plagues the nation. Those are not the words of high drama or a flight of wild fantasy. The dislocation of the American Dream, if it ever really existed beyond the suburbs of post WW2, is reflected in the most profound fracture of power in the history of mankind. Most of the nation's wealth, assets (natural and artificial), and opportunities are concentrated in the hands of a few thousand families and persons. These are exactly the people who have a disproportionate amount of access to and influence upon the criminal justice and political systems, and there is no reason to believe these kind hearted folks are going to part with the lucre and power anytime soon. Why would they?

There is, however, more to understanding the disparities of justice than plopping the blame on the front lawns of the rich. Besides, we continue to celebrate the cult of billionaires as a model of the true American success story. We need to explore other reasons. Those other reasons, noted elsewhere, include the social caste system of education, racism, poverty, and the very imperfect administration of justice, among many others...

The very good news, however, is that prospects for change in the criminal justice system do exist but those will be hard-earned reforms. They are most definitely not for the faint of heart. Yet - maybe we can pull it off. A good start might be opening the closed mind and the shuttered heart. Besides, think of how impressed your friends will be when you trot out some pithy Latin phrase to your friends at the coffee shop. Words spoken in a hushed, fervent tone of voice: "Daphne, Pardus hose est god's donum ut ortus imperium." Or - Panty hose is God's gift to birth control. I offer the Latin lessons free of charge...

Daniel S Campagna Ph.D.

Looking Elsewhere
Crime and Punishment; Fyodor Dostoyevsky

The Constitutional Convention: A Narrative History from the Notes of James Madison

www.ncjrs.gov

http://www.pbs.org/wgbh/pages/frontline/gunned/down

www.bjs.gov

# Two

## Evil is as Evil Does

*"Did I do anything wrong today," he said, "or has the world always been like this and I've been too wrapped up in myself to notice?"*

Douglas Adams, The Hitchhiker's Guide to the Galaxy

Before we move into the nuts and bolts of crime and justice in America, we must first put things into proper context, set the stage so to speak, and move some props about. Let us therefore first put all of the cards on the topic of what we are talking about. Felonies and misdemeanors. Violations of people, property, spirit and soul. All crimes must fall within two broad standards known as mala in se and mala prohibita.

Mala in se - This refers to an act that is "evil unto itself". Or simply put, these are behaviors so nasty and vile that even an intoxicated hedge fund CEO, anexoric Swedish fashion model in tow, would not touch them without advice of counsel. Psycho and sociopaths relish these acts; they are gourmands at the great banquet of human suffering adding an extra pinch of their own demented vision to the recipe:

> *"Ariel Castro of Cleveland was convicted of kidnapping three women and chained them in the basement for 10 years. In addition he was found guilty of multiple rapes, beatings, and impregnating one woman five times, punching her in the stomach until she miscarried."*

Mr. Castro, by the way, committed suicide in jail possibly from a guilty conscience although that seems unlikely. His death is no loss to society and this case makes one wonder:

A. What could have made Castro so devoted to these horrible mala in se crimes? He and Mr. Jeffrey Dahmer and others of their ilk remain enigmas to behavioral investigators.
B. What did the eulogy sound like, e.g. gone but not forgotten?
C. How could three women vanish for a decade without the police being able to track down even a single one?

Clearly, and this is admittedly in hindsight, the Cleveland detective bureau might have fumbled the case. Ten years missing? Time to consult the local psychics because evidently reading Tarot Cards and palms would, at worse, produce the same investigative outcomes which is to say – NAFT – Not a Fucking Thing or, at best, some vague directions for fresh lines of inquiry. By the way, the Cleveland incident with Castro is not a one off. Variations on these themes of sexual domination, wholesale destruction of families, and other mala in se acts, are abundant in the annals of crime in America and show no indication of slowing down. As enthusiasts of abnormal behaviors, American consumers can simply check in with the news for their daily dose of mala in se.

Murder (certain types), sex with the dead (come now, necrophilia is really not a hobby), cannibalism (say, how does one properly sauté thigh of grandpa?), and sleeping with your sister or brother are ready examples of mala in se acts. The latter instance is a big no-no. Incest has a few noteworthy exceptions in history (see British royalty, Aztec bluebloods and Egyptian pharaohs). Incest also has a biological basis – it helps spawn two-headed idiots who become kings with I.Q.'s that plummet faster than a defective NASA launch. On an upside, autistic squirrel boys and girls pop up from these unhappy unions of eggs and sperm that can recite the math tables backwards while spinning like a toy top. That is mala in se. Like believing in the power of the ballot box, it is hard to imagine a society progressing beyond racism, religious and sexual intolerance as long as mala in se thrives. Nothing good ever comes from an act of mala in se.

Besides, mala in se is nasty stuff and who's going to clean up the mess? Commit an act of mala in se, such as screwing the livestock (bestiality) on some sunny spring morning and see what happens. Granted, Betsy the cow has such inviting eyes but get caught with your pants down standing on a three-legged stool and you will find your mugshot draped across the mighty, mighty Interweb. Probably with the caption, "Garsh Petey! I thought it was love!" and you wearing a very goofy grin.

> *"Cirilo Castillo Jr., 45, was arrested in February in Edinburg, Texas, but a charge was not filed until June, apparently because prosecutors were awaiting Castillo's recovery from a broken leg. He had been found in a barn after trying to have sex with a horse -- three years after having been convicted of a similar crime (and warned, at that time, to stay away from the Edinburg farm). The broken leg happened, prosecutors said, because in the February incident, the horse kicked him."*
>
> *MySanAntonio.com, 6-10-2015*

So, word to the wise – avoid any and all acts of mala in se unless you belong to a fanatical religion or political ideology (Hello ISIS / Ku Klux Klan / Aryan Brotherhood / Bloods, Crips, and other gangs / Westboro Baptist Church) in which case those guys (true believers) are Zen masters of the Art of Inhumanity and Disinformation. Mala in se is their bread and butter lifestyle. Those folks invent new ways to offend humanity such as killing cartoonists who draw caricatures of Mohammed and blowing up train stations, mosques, and schools. Furthermore, they hurt defenseless people, especially woman because they refuse to be treated as sexual property with third-class citizen rights. And gay or black people? Let me personalize this bit. You nasty bastards drag them behind pickup trucks, hang them on barbed wire fences in the grasslands of Wyoming, set them afire, or toss acid on them. You hate and plot and destroy like Godzilla on a weekend booze bender in Tokyo. You rationalize the collapse of your moral core with the most ludicrous ideas. You spew the ideology of destruction and practice the nihilistic behaviors so common to mala in se. The ironic thing is – you are the problem, not those you prey upon. In my fantasy world, which includes balloons and confetti and orange unicorns, all of the mala in se people are launched into deep space for a one-way journey to anyplace else but planet earth. We would be a much improved species.

On the other hand, selling your brother's sports card collection while he is at work is wrong in itself (joke – it's not, just a shitty trick to play unless he can establish ownership in which case you committed fraud maybe, theft for certain). That leads us to the second classification of criminal forms commonly called mala prohibita. Mala prohibita means, in a small nutshell, that some behavior is made illegal by law.

Most deviant acts are "banned by popular consensus" e.g. Congressmen who solicit homosexual acts while sitting on the toilet in a public restroom, but until an act is actually put into law, the behavior is not a crime. Sure, we may resent throwing away a vote on some 50'ish, fat cat, corporate owned federal legislator sitting on a public toilet trying to hook up with a quick blow job. But hey! – that's democracy with all of its delicious perks! What better way to make a BFF? Besides, a very stout argument could be made that voting for the incumbent political hack is simply a definition of insanity – doing the same thing over and over hoping for a better result. So, we must go further with mala prohibita and dig deeper as to what makes these crimes different from mala in se. All criminal laws must have two key pieces:

(1) Definition (elements) of the crime and (2) Penalty.

Ergo, thus, and okey dokey – all crimes are inked in law. Each has a definition with elements or pieces of the crime, and a penalty for people who are convicted of violating that law. We normally sort out these various acts as crimes of property and/or person. Many crimes have a touch of both. Fraud, burglary, beating the devil out of someone, and dumping millions of gallons of crude oil into the Gulf of Mexico (thanks British Petroleum and you are always welcome to come back and finish cleaning up your eco-disaster), releasing methyl isocyanate gas, a pesticide that injured 500,000 people in India (Union Carbide) or spilling coal ash into the water table and wells in North Carolina (Duke Energy) –"oh, so that's why our share values dropped, and the drinking water smells like a Cairo sewer drain, eh?"- are examples of acts made illegal through legislation that affect person and property. You might think that poisoning the citizenry is a form of mala in se, whether it involves toxins released by manufacturers floating in the wind and into homes and workplaces, or poisons (arsenic, strychnine, chemical fertilizers, liquid manure run-offs ) seeping in to the water tables, would constitute an evil in itself but not necessarily so. We are, after all, referring to corporations and in America, that red, white and blue citadel of the free market, corporations routinely get a pass for evil acts. Think of it as a "get out of jail almost always" card available to most companies regardless of how dangerous or fatal their products and practices.

You might think, for example, that building a product that kills consumers (intentional homicide) should be an act of mala in se. Hmm, not so much...

> *"According to the Center for Auto Safety, 303 people were killed in crashes of certain now-recalled General Motors vehicles where the airbags did not deploy in time."*

Mala prohibita, on the other hand, is often adjusted over time and each state has a different definition for the various types of criminal acts. Each state and the federal government, moreover, organize the acts of mala in se and mala prohibita by categories known as felony and misdemeanor with levels of degree and difference between and within them.

Felony – universally known as a serious or major crime.

So, for example, if you whack somebody with a Louisville Slugger baseball bat – it's been known to happen – that would be a case of aggravated assault (felony) or possibly AWDW (Assault with a Deadly Weapon). Clearly the potential for major harm, possibly death or permanent brain damage, exists. That's what defines the word aggravated. The presence of a serious weapon such as a bat or knife raises the potential for "grievous harm" aka the victim wakes up below ground. Penalties are on a sliding scale ranging from - "Community service for six weeks. The victim is a notorious asshole and needed some enlightenment" to "Well, the court agrees that the victim was a thoughtless, selfish, racist gorm but you can't hit him for being ignorant or else we would run out of politicians and newscasters and celebrities. 10 years of hard time for you."

Depending on the state, felonies are structured by level, class or category of harm. Not all felonies are created equal in that regard and a criminal code logically recognizes the need to separate felonies (and penalties) on the basis of exactly what happened and the consequences for it. Plus, lest we forget, conviction of a felony means you must mark "Yes!" on all future employment applications thus stigmatizing you until death do you part from us. Looks like a career in whipping up pancakes and eggs at a greasy spoon diner lies ahead, at less than minimum wage and no benefits. Coffee, by the way, is free.

Misdemeanor – crimes of lesser harm

Now flip the coin and replace the Slugger with a foam bat. Keep smacking your neighbor (the one whose five dogs never stop barking) over the head. Go ahead. I'll wait. No, sorry, I almost forgot. This is a visual society. I will record the incident for you on YouTube, Twitter, Reddit, BiteMe, etc. and anyplace I can use the material to get loads of Likes and Thumbs Up. Of course those videos will be introduced as material evidence at your court hearing. Hitting that nasty shit-bum neighbor is a case of simple assault (misdemeanor). The penalties will be lightweight aka no jail time.

"Unless" you have mastered the ancient Kung Fu art of deadly foam bats, odds are you will be charged with a misdemeanor. That is bad for you and the dogs still bark. Relax. The worst that will happen is probably going to be a restraining order and a small fine. A restraining order is a judgment from the court that says "curb yourself" and stay away from the victim and his yapping mutts. Also known as a paper wall of almost no use or value in protecting you from further harm except to create a paper trail. These documents can be placed in your official court file after the funeral (yours) or the next beating from the person(s) aka spouse, who was supposed to stay away from you. Try waving that restraining order in front of the offender and see how that works out. It is akin to running with the bulls in Pamplona with you wearing a bright red clown suit and floppy shoes.

In this case of the five mutts and foam bat, let's pretend that you were a bit inebriated and not in full control of your otherwise sterling good judgment. That is known as a potentially mitigating circumstance. If the judge and prosecutor accepts your special line of bullshit – "That damn Mojito just knocked me sideways, your honor!" you may get off with virtually no punishment except an apology to the victim and a reminder to "drink responsibly" in the future. Otherwise, expect a fine and some serious frowning from the judge and your neighbor aimed at you in court. You can live with that. Next time, do the smart thing and open a hole in the fence for the dogs to escape. You are welcome.

There are levels of criminal codes – Federal, state(s), and local codes known as ordinances. The latter involves regulations designed by each community in such matters as public safety, zoning, and public order crimes e.g. loud parties. My small town in Missouri, for example, had an ordinance dealing with horseshit and tie-ups for Amish buggies. Yeah, riveting stuff. We also had a town drunk who enjoyed firing his gun through his trailer roof and bicycling around town while shouting at people. And, one more memory trip – a militia nut job had a very large tree growing through a car on his lawn. He threatened to kill anyone who tried to move the car ("infringement of a citizen's rights by local government"). There were local rules banning these behaviors but unless the acts were a direct threat to someone, many communities exercise their own version of laissez faire law. Fingers crossed, in other words, that the shitty neighbor(s) move to Memphis or fall into a deep alcoholic coma (same thing).

It helps to do a simple comparison of the Federal and state laws with their definitions and penalties. Doing so will give the reader a clearer idea, hopefully, of the distinctions and reasoning behind such laws. For instance, let us ponder a question that is never brought up at bar mitzvahs or game shows:

> Q: *"What does a cattle rustler have in common with a pirate?"*
> A: *10 years to Life.*

In Wyoming, cattle rustling is a felony or major property offense and is listed as follows:

> *Wyoming Criminal Code: 6-3-413. <u>Rustling</u>*

Definition/Elements: A person who knowingly takes or exercises unlawful control over or makes an unauthorized transfer of an interest in any horse, mule, sheep, cattle, buffalo or swine with the purpose of depriving the lawful owner or possessor of the same is guilty of livestock rustling.

Penalty: Livestock rustling is a felony punishable by imprisonment for not more than ten (10) years, a fine of not more than ten thousand dollars ($10,000.00), or both.

It makes sense that a western rural state like Wyoming would frown on the theft of livestock. 10 years in prison is a long stretch for hoisting someone's livestock.

The Federal Criminal Code, on the other hand, has different definitions and penalties and, in some case, crimes that would not be needed in some or all states. Such as piracy (not the music file stealing type). Before slipping into your favorite

Blackbeard costume with knee boots and eye patch, take a look at what is in store for you and your swashbuckling buccaneers. Note: this advice does not apply to Somali pirates. They hear their own drummers and this usually includes access to rocket propelled grenade launchers. Also, be mindful that these two laws have nothing to do with cruise ships and getting screwed (not the fun way) by passengers and staff on those love boats of high sea adventure.

*18 U.S.C. § 1652 : US Code - Section 1652: Citizens as pirates*

Definition/Elements: Whoever, being a citizen of the United States, commits any murder or robbery, or any act of hostility against the United States, or against any citizen thereof, on the high seas, under color of any commission from any foreign prince, or state, or on pretense of authority from any person, is a pirate, and ...

Penalty:…shall be imprisoned for life.

*18 U.S.C. § 1659 : US Code - Section 1659: Attack to plunder vessel*

Definition: Whoever, upon the high seas or other waters within the admiralty and maritime jurisdiction of the United States, by surprise or open force, maliciously attacks or sets upon any vessel belonging to another, with an intent unlawfully to plunder the same, or to despoil any owner thereof of any moneys, goods, or merchandise laden on board thereof, shall be…

Penalty:...fined under this title or imprisoned not more than ten years, or both.

How can this be? Just accept it. Each state has its own communal sense of wrongful behavior. The federal government has jurisdiction (authority) over a wide range of acts and duties not delegated to the states. This includes such things as the national defense, weights and measures, surveillance of all digital transmissions (federal government), highways, and the Library of Congress Book Return SWAT Team. Yeah, no such thing as that last entity but many a librarian must get some very wet dreams over the thought of police raids on book thieves. "Hands in the air you bastards! Where are you stashing the 4th edition of Huck Finn! ZZZZZZTTT! Taser the bastard again, Frank!" Now you know what my fertile, if skewed, imagination looks like when it has too much free time.

A truly smart criminal, oxymoron aside, would stop by the local library and review the criminal codes. Picture our suave budding criminal neophyte - Tyrick DeMarcus Octavian Smith, the burglar, perusing the state legal codes. Picture his earnest brows furrowed with concentration (still working on his GED) as he sorts out the language of law and numbers higher than a single digit. Naturally, this does not apply to white-collar crooks and cyber thugs. The former have their GED, a smartphone, speed dial to their shysters, and a stack of someone else's credit cards. Cyber crooks, on the other hand, are very, very difficult to catch and even more unlikely to be prosecuted. In my jaded opinion, these identity thieving, bank account draining, information hijackers need to be relocated to the Everglades with a spoon, flashlight, bug spray and ankle monitor for three months. Sounds like the makings of a terrific Reality Show – Cyber Thieves versus Nature in the Wild!" The survivor either gets airlifted to a transgender clinic or, in the case of a happy Burmese python – the snake is treated to an entrée of adult male (or female, no need to discriminate). I bet consumers would pay a hefty ticket price to watch cyber thieves (and white collar criminals) get swallowed, ass first, down the snake's gullet. Yum! Pay-for-view television gala! Whew! Let me pause and get a drink of water.

Right, back to our protagonist. Tyrick. "Eureka!" he shouts, because in my fantasy offenders like Tyrick speak in clichés - "If I crack the electronics warehouse in Alabama the penalty could be up to 10 years for a first conviction. In Maine the most I could get is 2-5 years. When is the next Greyhound bus to Bangor?" That is known as time-tested learning. Same crime, different time. Lots of reasons for those sentence disparities which we will consider later. The good news for police is that the "average" or run-of-the-mill crook is about as intelligent as a ceramic lawn ornament. Not the cheery gnome type, more like the hostile, glaring red eyes of a constipated bulldog chewing on broken glass.

"Christopher Wallace has reached legendary show-off status. Being sought in connection with a January burglary, he went to his home in Fairfield, Maine -- and posted on the Snapchat site that that's where he was. Police arrived and, during their canvass, noticed a brand-new Snapchat post from

Wallace - mischievously writing that police were in his home right then, searching for him, but that he was cunningly hiding in a cabinet. Police opened the cabinet and arrested him."

Associated Press via Morning Sentinel (Waterville, Maine), 3-24-2015

It pays to note, at this point, that someone can be arrested for a crime that is planned but not fully executed as demonstrated by the artful chimney thief: *"A 17-year-old burglary suspect was pulled from a chimney by firefighters after being stuck there for more than 10 hours in a home in Norcross, Atlanta."*

Otherwise known as an inchoate (incomplete) crime, this is a very necessary piece of the criminal laws. Society does not really want to wait until the crime has been completed before making an arrest; that's common sense. In the case of the artful chimney thief the charge would likely be attempted breaking and entering or a version thereof. Plus an extra charge for being so blatantly stupid.

What's that I hear you say? Didn't do anything wrong? Yes, you did. You are a law-abiding, god-fearing (pick a god, it doesn't matter to me, they all tend to wear the same aftershave) upright citizen cut from the broad tapestry that says police are omnipotent. "Officer, how can I help? No sir, I am innocent and at this moment you are my God and parent. Guide me." No worries, you may still be liable (responsible). Clink, Clink, go the handcuffs. Get your indigent, confused self in the patrol car. There are, in fact, crimes of omission which is to say -

> Failing to act (omission) when a lawful duty to do so is in place (law) is a common event.

Child neglect, not filing income taxes, failing to help at the scene of an accident (Good Samaritan Law depending on the state), and many others are ready examples of crimes of omission. These laws involving acts of omissions include, of course, elements and penalties. Let me be very clear about omissions; not doing something can be a crime. Add to this mélange a concept called strict liability. Simply put, this means there are no acceptable excuses for not obeying certain laws such as driving responsibly and paying taxes. All competent adults are supposed to know about these laws.

Context matters when we discuss laws and crimes. Public opinions, religious (read=white Christianity) values of dubious merit, political parties with their agendas, special interest groups, all have their hands in the swirling kettle of moonshine known as making laws. Until very recently, for instance, gay relationships / marriages / adoptions were generally not afforded protection of law.

That condition has clearly changed for the better much to the anger and dismay of often divorced Christians preaching the sanctity of marriage. People were prosecuted, incarcerated, and fired for their status as gay, lesbian, or transgender human beings. In other words, these were people seen as "different", outside mainstream America and deserving of punishment and isolation. Context does matter more than we may want to admit. Laws define crimes and these laws change with time but traditionally have lagged behind shifting times and expectations. Contraceptives, abortions, alcohol use, interracial marriages, casino gambling outside of Nevada, and voting twice in one election (unless you were a resident of Cook County, Illinois) and marijuana consumption, were all illegal upon a time.

The most common tactic needed to change laws is to volunteer to break the law under challenge. The citizen in those situations must assume all of the risks and costs for doing so because a tsunami sized storm of normality, convention, bigotry and social bias will be arrayed against him/her. See Roe v. Wade for starters. Don't even contemplate this step unless you are prepared to lose everything in the process with a Pyrrhic Victory (See Rosa Parks and Claudette Colvin seated in the front of a segregated bus) in the hopes of taking a symbolic stand on a cause near and dear to you. Better yet, bribe the zoning inspector or politician or buy a judge. This is a faster, more efficient approach if you have the chink to put down under the table. Perhaps the most efficacious method for enacting change in the criminal justice systems is to simply bribe the legislators via campaign contributions and political action committees, hand them a pre-drafted bill, and tell them to get it passed with no excuses. Or just commit a crime to showcase the unfairness of the criminal justice system.

All of these variations, by the way, of what is or is not a crime can cause migraines and nervous tics in anyone unfamiliar with the rule of law. This concept is based on the idea that laws, not whims or groups, should be the bedrock of a government and its structures including criminal justice. The hope is that those laws will be fundamentally fair, equally applied, and amenable to change when required. The fact that this expectation is routinely shattered on the hard rocks of self-interest and the tides of misfortune (nautical references, no extra charge) is nothing new. Furthermore, it is not enough to behave. Save that advice for children. What does matter is awareness; here is a very practical formula to figure out what type of crime you may have committed and whether you need to call a lawyer for advice or flee to Honduras (no worries about extradition.)

## Formula: What in the Hell Did I Just Do?

Actus Reus (criminal act) + Mens Rea (Evil Intent or Mind) + Concurrence (act and mind occurring together) = Crime. Insert your act with your state of mind and shake the test tube and see what bubbles up. All three pieces of this formula must be present to decipher exactly what you are going to be arrested for (or not). Let's use a simple, frequently repeated incident to demonstrate the formula in action.

"Mustang Sally is a cashier at a big box store. She needs money for yoga pants, the type that leaves nothing to the imagination and smell like very old fish within days of wearing. Ignoring the cameras (mens rea) poised above the registers, Sally dips her hand into the till (actus reus) and removes

$100 (concurrence), hoping the shift manager will rack the loss up to a miscount of receipts. Mustang Sally is guilty of theft (misdemeanor) under $100 and will be fired and have to pay restitution which is financially unlikely for a broke, unemployed clerk. The court's judgment will be a mark against her credit rating, an additional penalty. "

A side point is that employee theft is widespread and a key factor in the failure of small businesses. The formula works for most crimes. For example, calculate the outcome (act, mind, concurrence) with the following incident involving a "sock offender". Fans of Freud and Kraft Ebbing will be nodding their heads in approval:

> *"James Dowdy, 43, on parole for an earlier sock theft, was arrested once again in Belleville, Illinois, after police received reports of socks missing in burglaries. Authorities said Dowdy had been involved in" other types of sock-related incidents (and) using socks in an inappropriate and obscene manner, "but details were not reported."*
> *WFTS-TV (Tampa), 3-16-2015, Belleville News-Democrat, 5-20-2015*

As indicated in the above example, Motive or "why" is not, contrary to crime shows, a requirement of proof within this formula. It can help but oftentimes motive is a bonus at trial e.g. "I needed the money for meth, so I had to have it." Perhaps not the most inspired statement from a defendant but honest in its utterance. The motive of drug addicts, whether doctors or street users, is evident; the neurochemical basis of addiction and dependency overrides other considerations of ethical conduct, restraint, empathy for others, and so forth. Or, as conservative commenters would argue – "The guy is a piece of shite meth head and it is all his fault. He had a choice not to do it!" So motive is handy to have for use at court but not essential. Forget the rubbish you see in the television crime shows about motive.

# Maxim

The construction of laws is almost wholly cued to the preferred morals and financial interests of the reigning government (federal and state) groups and wealthiest people. That is not news. That is history repeating itself. What is different now is the hard fact that the bulk of our nation's wealth, assets, raw materials, and capital are vested in the hands of less than 10% of the population. These families, officials and corporate "entrepreneurs" can decide what is or is not a crime e.g. easing of dumping restrictions for toxic waste, minimum security camps for convicted white collar criminals, bankrolling the political aspirations of an ambitious prosecutor or judge, and so forth. They do so by buying the people who make the laws, set the criminal codes and decide the penalties. They do so by catering to special interests. Again, nothing new and who cares? Also, these same persons and groups have an "agenda", a vision for America that invariably takes us all the way back to the notion of finding the least advantaged groups in society. The next step is to download most of society's shoulder aches and pains, its STD's, cramping and dismal swamp ailments upon those folks.

To help spread this vision of fear and justice denied, the media shapes popular impressions of who commits crimes. The fear machine is constantly cranked up to levels of paranoia not seen since Japan bombed Pearl Harbor on December 7, 1941. The stately, most recognizable images of crime in America today are young black males in hoodies and male Muslim citizens who have decided to commit a crime in the guise of religious righteousness (read=nobody loves me but my mother and Allah and neither is returning my phone calls since I bought a handgun, grew a beard, and started sexting stupid American teenage girls to join my jihad). The hoodie, however, remains the dominant image. But it does not typify crime in this country, nor really explain who the major culprits are in America. No, that image is owned by the white guy with a razor haircut, two-button suit, and buddies in the boardroom. Check these vultures out carefully. Then check for your wallet.

Robbing a bank, for instance, is a crime that yields about $5,000 (chump change) on the average. Bank robbery is a crime of the addict, the desperate, and the end-of-the-road kind of person. Short-term gains that are erased by years of lost revenue in prison. It can produce a 15-year stretch in a federal prison. While 15 years is ample time to catch up on one's reading and pick up a trade such as fermenting grapes and yeast in condoms to make that very delicate wine known as Exploding Eyeballs, the typical bank robber is not a shrewd fund investor.

Embezzling from the same bank for millions, on the other hand, and stock manipulations is likely to produce zero prison time. Remember that entourage of high-priced lawyers who specialize in insulating rich assholes from the consequences of jail time and a bad reputation? There we go. It is a yellow (gold) brick road for those smiling patricians of industry. At that rarified level lady justice is bent over the dais, skirt up, grunting, and the scales of right and wrong are kicked across the marbled courtroom floor. Plus, those very same thieves emerge with money and reputation intact (maybe a fine just to show that society means business pardon the pun), at least among their fellow whore mongers of industry.

> *"Faced with a government fee accepted by most real estate investors who view it as a routine cost of doing business, wealthy Arizona investor Wayne Howard balked. Instead of the ordinary filing-fee rate of $50 for registering a property deed, he demanded that all 2,922 of his deeds be recorded for $500, and when the Pinal County treasurer turned him down, he told the official he would simply use his pull in the legislature to change the law and get his 99.6 percent discount that way."*
>
> *(He almost succeeded. The bill passed the state Senate and was favored in the House, but after the*

*Arizona Republic newspaper exposed Howard's imperial move, it failed, 30-28.)*

*[Arizona Republic, 3-18-2015]*

Mala in se or mala prohibita, it does not matter. There are actually three tiers of crimes – those for the poor, those for the rapidly vanishing middle class, and those for the uber rich. Guess which tier gets its collective heads beat in with the gavel of justice?

Looking Elsewhere
One Flew Over the Cuckoo's Nest; Ken Kesey

MacBeth; William Shakespeare

# Three

*"In a closed society where everybody's guilty,*
*the only crime is getting caught. In a world*
*of thieves, the only final sin is stupidity."*

Hunter S. Thompson

I shake my head as I write this passage. People are so curiously predictable. We all commit crimes, sometimes a big boner of a crime aka DUI, cheating on income taxes, illegal drug usage, lying under oath, raping an intoxicated co-ed at a party (he said, she said), ad infinitum. And enough misdemeanors to form a chain of people that links all the way to the furthest point of the Milky Way Galaxy or at least to the black hole in the center. I did the math, trust me. It is a long chain stretched a tad thin.

Give it up gang. We - you, me, and mom and dad have all sampled mala prohibita acts to greater or lesser degrees and that is not necessarily a bad thing. Time for "true confessions" anonymously. Don't send me your admissions of guilt and critical remarks nor please do not act like an atomic dickhead with your vehement denials. In fact, the louder you protest your innocence the more suspicious I become. And try not to throw your hands up in the air beseeching some God to forgive you. Take some degree of ownership – "Yes Lord, Allah, Thor. I did strike my spouse and maybe I should have not used full force but it was for her/his own good. Damn! My fist really hurts from that last punch."

Indeed, take responsibility for being a criminal. We all break the law. Our state and county governments break the law. The federal government breaks the laws. Our religions break the law. Our celebrities, athletes, religious leaders, and heroes break the laws often and routinely. It is often unavoidable for reasons we will examine. So, inhale deeply and let out a foggy breadth of relief. It's not just you; it is every legally competent adult (and juvenile) who can distinguish between right and wrong, broadly defined. That in no way makes it AOK. It depends entirely on the type and degree of one's behavior. It is a far stretch, for instance, from placing a $5 illegal wager on the Superbowl outcome versus prowling the streets of southwest Chicago (82 shootings, 14 deaths during the 4th of July weekend, 2015) looking for someone from a rival gang worth shooting. Better idea – remove the bullets from the gun, dump the gun in the Chicago River (to join thousands of other weapons), go home and read a book. Nobody dies and you learn something new. That is called a true win-win situation in criminal justice.

# Legacy

As a culture that is only 350 years or so, the United States, its people, institutions, and groups, have embraced violence in a myriad of shapes without hesitation and often with open arms. Like any collective memory it is common to shove the unpleasantness of past crimes and hatreds into the dusty recesses of textbooks and official archives to be periodically resurrected as a film or "new study" about why and when and how our society has been addicted to and in love with the practice of violence. It is a love affair that rivals the Siege of Troy and Romeo and Juliet, neither of which you may recall ended particularly well.

Breaking the law is part of the American heritage, an integral aspect of our culture. We landed on the east coast 350 years past and starting banging away at the natives with muskets and cocks and smallpox riddled blankets ("Happy Thanksgiving you red skinned motherfuckers!"), opening up the slave pens ("hmm…I'll buy that big buck. Let's see his teeth."), hiring thousands of Chinese coolies ("the dregs of Asia or yellow monkeys") to lay track for the transcontinental railroad (Manifest Destiny) and so onward and upward our civilization progressed. You may have noticed that progress is invariably at someone else's expense e.g. put over 100,000 American citizens of Japanese descent into internment camps during WW2. In fact it would be depressingly easy to exhaust the rest of this book with a catalog of such crimes conducted by "us" against "them". "Them" includes women, children, minorities, illegal immigrants, homosexuals/lesbians, atheists, inmates, homeless, Native Americans, juvenile delinquents, mentally ill, physically handicapped, low I.Q.'s, the poor, and so forth. America has been routinely whopping the collective bodies and spirits of these people since they exited the womb with public shaming, exile, torture, lynching, beatings, discriminatory laws and regulations, scientific experiments (eugenics) and punishments based on one's status rather than due process. No, this is not that type of narrative. Instead of sampling from that very yummy box of historical nuggets, let's try a different tack to appreciate social deviance and crime.

Read the tick list below and see how many of these criminal or deviant activities you may have indulged in, you know, just for a lark. I will stand in as your father confessor. Have a seat. Draw the curtain shut and close the damn door! Don't be concerned that I am not wearing pants.

"Father Daniel, I am a virtuous person but since my last confession I may have been involved in some of the following activities:"

Distracted Driving; constantly speed and drive like a spasmodic twat on the highway while texting and chatting with all four hundred of your closest friends. This habit kills an estimated 3,500 people, mostly teenagers, and injures tens of thousands more ever year.

> *"1) Joseph Forren, 21, with a .172 blood alcohol level, plowed into a pickup truck in April in Trumbull, Connecticut (though with no serious injuries). Police said Forren's cellphone on the seat still displayed a current text message, "Don't drink and drive ... Dad.""*

*(2) According to police records released in April, Mila Dago (now 24 and awaiting trial for DUI manslaughter) was trading sarcastic texts with her ex-boyfriend that night in August 2013 while barhopping (later, registering .178 blood alcohol), and as she ran a red light, smashed into a pickup truck, injuring herself badly and her friend in the passenger seat fatally. According to the police report, her last text to the ex- boyfriend (three minutes earlier) was "Driving drunk woo ... I'll be dead thanks to you."*

*Connecticut Post (Bridgeport, 4-27-2015), Miami Herald, 4-30-2015*

A worthy side note: In December 2012, "phoners" sent / received more than 171 billion text messages in the US. It is no wonder the National Security Agency's budget keeps expanding to meet the demands of so many busy beaver texters and talkers. But for the rest of us, 2013 was a bad year to give up walking because:

Large truck crashes and deaths: 3,964 people killed and an estimated 95,000 people injured in crashes involving large trucks. In the United States, an estimated 342,000 large trucks were involved in police-reported traffic crashes during 2013. In short, there are oodles of dangerous truck drivers tooling down the roads of America.

Vehicle crashes and deaths: 5,687,000 police-reported crashes, resulting in 32,719 people killed and an estimated 2,313,000 people injured.

Bicyclists: 743 bicyclists killed and an estimated 48,000 injured in motor vehicle crashes.

Motorcyclists: 4,668 motorcyclists killed in motor vehicle traffic crashes. There were an estimated 88,000 motorcyclists injured.

80 = Average number of people killed on US roads each day

Non-fatal crashes annually: 5.4 Million

And, of course, you my precious would never speed or drive while distracted, or act in any reckless way behind the wheel. That is what OTHERS do. The primary laws of physics (velocity, stopping distance, rate of impact and ouch!) do not apply to you. Besides, in your world of calculated probability, fatalities and accidents, aside from the wee bumper thumpers, are things to gawk at as you slow down to look at the carnage, maybe take a few quick selfies to send to friends. "Oooohh, somebody fucked up, eh? Is that a child in the backseat of that crushed mom's mini-van? Poor thing. Ah well, thank Buddha I would never act like that! "The odds are always in your favor, much like the Powerball Lottery.

Cheated the federal government of its share of taxes every April 5th. There are an estimated 1.6 million citizens who cheat on their taxes each year. That seems like a rather high level of tax evasion, eh Binky? This number does not include the number of intentionally false tax returns filed by identity thieves, inmates, and assorted crooks. A rough estimate of losses due to their activities range from $20-$50 billion annually. How best to describe this dilemma of citizens routinely cheating the government of its rightful taxes? Relax, the rich pay far, far less in taxes and cheat by shifting their wealth to offshore investments and foreign banks. This number does not include the IRS employees who defraud the government, to wit:

> *"About three-fourths of the 1,580 IRS workers found to have deliberately attempted to evade federal income tax during the last 10 years have nonetheless retained their jobs, according to a May report by the agency's inspector general. Some even received promotions and performance bonuses (although an internal rule, adopted last year, now forbids such bonuses to one adjudged to owe back taxes)."*
> *Associated Press via Yahoo.com, 5-6-2015*

$270,000,000,000 = Amount lost annually by the U.S. Treasury due to unreported income.

http://news.yahoo.com/4-billion-bogus-tax-refunds-growing-problem-163413856--finance.html

<u>Crossed the drinking line at a party and drove home</u>. Or high, drugged, or some cocktail mix of the moment. In all fairness, however, the road, however, did seem a bit edgy and difficult to follow. But, just this one time. Looks like the highway department forgot to paint straight lines on the road. Better call them in the morning and notify them of the problem.

Several million drivers are estimated in 2013 to have operated a vehicle while under the influence of alcohol and/or drugs.

Stole property or committed fraud as an employee. Tools, copy paper, furniture, stuff you need and besides, you work hard and deserve some bennies (free stuff). Hey – forget the corporation, right? They will never notice the stuff is missing. Submitted reimbursements for false business expenses? Three quick cocktails at lunch with a company vendor sound about fair, eh?

33% = Percent of all business bankruptcies caused by employee theft, the majority of which were small business operating a very slim operating and profit margin of 2%-3%. About one third of small businesses close every year due to employee theft and fraud.

37.5% = Percent of employees who have stolen at least twice from their employer.

7% = Percent of annual revenues lost to theft or fraud.

$50 Billion = Amount stolen annually from U.S. businesses by employees. This is considered to be a very low, conservative estimate. Some researchers argue that the actual losses are closer to $500 billion dollars annually. These losses, of course, are nominally inserted into operating budgets which is to say – the losses are passed on to the consumer whenever possible in the form of small service fees (fine print items), higher prices for necessities such as food and medicine, and so forth. This is referred to as a transferred cost. Translation: You stole from us. We steal it back.

Bullying: Sent threatening emails or revenge porn postings to anyone. Bullying and using the Interweb for defamation of character are some Grand Canyon sized shit crimes because it is too easy and convenient to do for those with hearts and minds full of spite and resentment. The hater is anonymous and uncensored unless one is able to get a court order to compel the Internet Service Provider (ISP) to reveal the sender's identity (very unlikely). Bullying is an offense which should be punishable by public stockades where victims can gather and offer advice such as – "You should move away from civilization and live in a cave." Or throw mud pies at them and, and…again, I get carried away by my boyish enthusiasm for doing something constructive when the criminal justice system does so very little with the crime of bullying.

It should not surprise the reader that popular social media sites, encrypted or not, and some porn sites are mediums wherein persons defame and shout a farrago of vile comments about someone else that include death and rape threats. Moreover, no rational person should be stunned by the statistical fact that the majority of these victims are females, people who are overweight or depressed, minorities, disabled, gay, and minors. Unfortunately, bullying is rarely subject to the full power and focus of the justice system. It is still viewed as a minor incident by police; on a scale of concern it rates just ahead of cybercrime e.g. identity theft, of which few departments are trained and equipped to address.

That, in no manner, excuses the lack of interest in this behavior. A bully is an assailant posed to strike; the Columbine High School shooters, for instance, were not helpless victims of any mistreatment at school or home. The popular notion that bullies act in response to their own victimizations is, at best, a flimsy explanation and more probably a convenient excuse for ghastly conduct. In groups such as gangs and at sporting events or parties, bullies are predators looking for prey. What, therefore, are some of the outcomes of bullying?

Commit or attempt suicide. Desperate, troubled and depressed people are especially vulnerable to bullying. Bullying has a direct cause-effect connection to suicides. Its rate of effectiveness varies by age group, intensity and type of bullying, and life circumstances e.g. homeless. For teenagers, the rate is notoriously high:

> *"Suicide is the third leading cause of death among young people, resulting in about 4,400 deaths per year, according to the CDC. For every suicide among young people, there are at least 100 suicide attempts. Over 14 percent of high school students have considered suicide, and almost 7 percent have attempted it."*

http://www.bullyingstatistics.org/content/bullying-and-suicide.html

Quit in despair. Quit school, quit work, develop addictions, and quit living a meaningful life. Unable to cope with the constant harassment of bullying and online extortion, the victim withdraws from society. Revenge porn, for instance, which involves taking intimate photos / videos of one's lover, then releasing them to the Interweb in revenge when the relationship sours can cause the victim to lose employment, damage one's reputation, generate mental illness, encourage suicide, and nurture a sense of helplessness. By the way, this behavior is not technically illegal in most states:

> *"Only 17 states have specific laws to protect against "revenge porn" (exposing ex-lovers' intimate images online as retaliation for a break-up), but a possible solution in the other states, reported CNN in April, is for the victim to file a "takedown" demand under the federal Digital Millennium Copyright Act, which would subject the avenger to penalties for not removing the images. However, to prove copyright, the victim must file copies of the bawdy images with the U.S. Copyright Office, increasing the victim's trauma."*
>
> *CNN Wire via WTKR-TV*
> *(Hampton Roads, Va.), 4-27-2015*

Solution: In the spirit of "Can Do!" which exemplifies the American working class ethic of fairness perhaps there is a relatively simple, inexpensive solution to bullying. How about - enact legislation that compels Internet Service Providers (ISP) and those who invite comments to reveal the identities online of alleged bullies and those who threaten us? Actually, I would prefer to see the identities of everyone revealed but that is my private dream world.

Some cyber critics have argued that another option might be to lure the hater to a cliff's edge for a selfie that ends in a 300-foot plummet onto the rocks of a Maine seaside cliff. Picture some Interweb troll pin wheeling to the ground from a cliff's edge, yelling "EEEEEWWWW!!!" or something equally pointless. Of course it would have to be recorded and shipped out to next of kin and the social media sites. Nothing in life should go unrecorded.

Threats: This is a variation of bullying, much more common and depressingly predictable and frequent. It is often a prelude to outright physical violence. For now, however, it is worth remembering that the issuance of a threat, by voice, gesture, etc. is a crime. It does not require the performance of the threat to qualify for an arrest. If the threat escalates to an act (actus reus), the prospect of harm escalates. That makes sense. Chuck in an alchemist blend of self-hatred and penis envy. The probability of a threat becoming a fact increases. The threat may be laden with such sexual overtones as "Shove it up your ass!", and an all-time favorite e.g. "Say, how's about I knock the stupid out of you?" The tone of these comments is contextual. Do you know anyone who has not ever issued a threat? Threats are usually the fuses that herald all sorts of physical assaults. Let us not lose that perspective. Threats, if activated, become assaults.

<u>Simple assaults</u>. No thoroughly accurate figure exists for this behavior. Our best guesses are derived from police reports and case records of child care services. We do know through the National Crime Victimization Survey (NCVS) that an enormous amount of crime goes unreported or underreported (minimized) in America. A simple assault does not yield severe physical harm or permanent injury. An easy example is a hot headed parent threatening her/his child accompanied by a loud smack to the child's face or a spanking. Spitting on someone is a simple assault as is having Aunt Beth kissing you without consent at a Xmas party. It is a matter, as noted earlier, of degree and type. Aunt Beth may smell like a Venice canal in midsummer but no harm, no foul. Spitting and biting, on the other hand, are more likely to hurt and result in some type of complaint. What we do know as a broad estimate that 4.7 million simple assaults occurred in 2012, accounting for the majority of victimizations in the United States.

As will be discussed later, simple assaults, when blended with the rates of unjustifiable aggravated assaults illustrate that Americans are aggressive louts. Apparently we are conditioned or maybe cerebrally hardwired or instinctively predisposed to diminish one another with physical force. To wit:

*Louie Sanchez, 31 and Marvin Norwood pled guilty to mayhem and beating Bryan Stow outside Dodger Stadium in 2011. Mr. Stow is permanently brain damaged and disabled from the beating. They beat the victim for being a San Francisco Giants fan. Neither assailant apologized at sentencing for their actions.*

# The Cheesecake Theory of Crime

The Sanchez – Norwood assault resulted in comparatively short prison terms of eight and four years respectively. Mr. Stow, on the other hand, must endure a lifetime of pain from the actions of these two sub-humans. This incident is included only for purposes of illustration and is, unfortunately, neither unique or a case study. It is meant to dramatize the basic difference between simple assaults, which most of us commit, and aggravated assaults which we do not (fortunately) commit with equal frequency.

Right, time to turn in your scorecard. The list includes common crimes such as threats and assaults,      bad driving, bullying and income tax evasion. Who among us, as mentioned in the <u>Book of Bob</u> (ancient tome from which all of the world's religious doctrines are distilled) has not "spoken in a manner that offends the public peace and made the maidenheads of many women tremble with fear?" In a society that criminalizes so many human behaviors through felonies, misdemeanors, and ordinances, it is simply not possible to traverse the plateaus of life without breaking a law. Or two. Hopefully, not with criminal intent and grievous harm such as staging dog fights, slashing the tires of someone who took your seat at a Florida bingo parlor ("my lucky chair!"), or stealing toys meant for needy children at Xmas. We ALL qualify for a hiccup or more when it comes to deviance and criminal acts, some more extreme and unnecessary than others. Mr. Jenkins, for instance, is a handy case in point:

*"Nikko Jenkins, convicted of murder in a 2013 spree and trying to avoid a scheduled sentencing hearing, recently*

*self-mutilated (for the second time), which he told a judge in Omaha, Nebraska, was evidence of his mental disorder that should render him ineligible for death row. Jenkins told the judge that a "serpent god" had ordered him to carve the "number of the beast" into his forehead, but apparently because Jenkins was looking into a mirror as he carved, his forehead display more resembled an upside-down 999 (or a lowercase ddd) than it did 666."*
*Omaha World-Herald, 4-17-2015*

So, why do we do break the law and how can such conduct be justified, if at all? We will examine some of the possible explanations about why in the coming chapter.

## Maxim

Criminology is the study of crime and deviance. It is an incomplete social science; much that needs to be discovered remains buried in sand somewhere. Other disciplines – sociology, psychology, anthropology – have joined in the hunt for answers as to why people commit crimes and they likewise have enjoyed marginal success. Crime (and victimization) is in all of us; no one gets a free pass on this behavior. Which may not, in fact, be a bad thing in some circumstances. Context is everything. As noted previously, great strides in human achievements within the arena of "right and wrong" often happen because someone was willing to break the law and accept the consequences in order to dramatize an injustice within the criminal justice system. But for working class stiffs who tried to walk the high wire of legality, the cross breezes of deviance can be tough to avoid. And that is a handy dandy metaphor to move into Chapter 4.

Looking Elsewhere
http://www.statisticbrain.com

www.nhtspa.gov/NCSA

http://www.bjs.gov/content/pub/pdf/cv12.pdf

http://newsoftheweird.com/

http://www.crimeinamerica.net/crime-rates-united-states/

http://www.meganmeierfoundation.org/statistics.html

http://www.cdc.gov/violenceprevention/pdf/bullying-sui-cide-translation-final-a.pdf

http://www.workplacebullying.org/tag/suicide/

# Four

## The Cheesecake Theory of Crime

*"The more things are forbidden, the*
*more popular they become."*

Mark Twain

We love to commit crimes and acts of deviance. It is a lifestyle and lifelong passion for some. Beneath the crusty façade of normality and righteous alignment with whatever passes as lawful behavior, we can be devious little pricks with very short-term consciences. Not everyone, of course, there are always exceptions BUT for the sake of argument – most of us. This section examines some of the more organized (as opposed to the shoot from the hip ideas of crime) theories of crime causation and deviance and ways in which we try to justify our acts. You will also be introduced to my own interpretation – The Cheesecake Theory of Crime.

# The Cheesecake Theory of Crime

A theory is simply a blueprint for discussing something, usually something complex like human behavior. No single theory can hope to satisfy our understanding of all types of crimes. People commit crimes for any wide number of reasons and it can depend on time, place, circumstance, culture (e.g. honor killings, voting for Donald Trump, leaving an infant on the roadside and driving away, poaching wildlife). We prefer simple explanations. Sometimes it is a simple matter such as a DUI that results in an accident without serious injuries. The driver was drunk, crashed, injuries, case closed. Other times, as when an elderly man lashes out at fellow "inmates" at a nursing home, the answer may be the by-product of many factors including poor circulation, the effects of cross medications, and the onset of dementia.

One problem is that the United States has criminalized so many human activities that it is virtually impossible to cross the richly textured landscape of life without tumbling into the "deviant zone." In that sense, we are undone by the enthusiasm of legislators who bring deeply rooted moral agendas to their posts e.g. "any woman who has an abortion needs to be treated as a Grade I felon and goddamn her selfish soul!!!" For the moment let us put aside the blindingly gross unfairness of men in power dictating what a woman can or cannot do with her body. Unless, of course, female lawmakers can do the same and require castration of unfit fathers? No, I thought not. But, I digress.

The zone of deviance is vast. It includes actions known as public order crimes. These are behaviors that interfere with the public peace such as disorderly conduct and so-called victimless crimes e.g. prostitution and gambling. A victimless crime presumes, as the title indicated, the absence of a victim. All parties to the activity are consenting adults. None wish to file a complaint against the other. On the other hand, go ahead and fart, tap dance, and shout out your name in public – those might be public order offenses. It depends on the tolerance of the police although none of those actions is technically a crime (unless your tap dancing is reminiscent of a grand mal seizure). Why did you do those things? You do not know. Maybe because it felt good or was fun at the time. I tried it once and by golly it did feel kind of pleasurable. The point being, however, that it does not take much to cross the very thin line between conformity, obedience and lawful behavior and enter the *deviant zone*. I do not recommend you put this to a test anytime soon unless you:

A. Have sufficient bail money (cash, no checks) or know someone who does to avoid being locked up or detained before your first hearing.
B. Are willing to enter the assembly line of case processing. Either agree to a plea deal or fight the charges and expect to lose.
C. Can risk becoming a docket number with the prospect of a lifelong stigma as a convicted misdemeanant or felon. Either way you are going to be lonely for a long while, because almost no one is going to be your advocate and your many "friends" on social media sites will flee your presence like

a case of rampaging chlamydia after a fraternity party. They figure that perhaps your situation could become contagious.

D. Are a minority who can dodge bullets, tasering, choke holds and serious beat downs off camera. If that is your case, then step up and join the ranks of modern superheroes (or super thugs).

If none of these options is appealing, be at ease. Remember, most encounters with the criminal justice system involve a traffic stop or call for help. Doing handstands on a hotel balcony railing during spring break in Florida, meanwhile, will draw the attention of the police. Or groping a fellow subway passenger during the morning commute to work. In either case, you will get a chance to test the effectiveness of the criminal justice system and your small role in it as a defendant.

Picture, therefore, a large, colorful carnival wheel with prizes in each slot. Except in this instance we place theories, not prizes, in the slots. Each slot has a different theory as to why we commit crimes. Some slots are narrower than others because they are CFOS (colossally full of shit) lacking even the whisper of proof or honest inquiry. The rest are of roughly even width. So step up and spin the magical wheel of theories. Watch as the wheel slaps gently against the flappers that slow down its momentum. Tick, tick,…we have a winner! Step up Classical Theorists and claim your prize!

Scholars and village idiots have been hammering at the gates of reason for centuries trying to decipher the secret code of crime and deviance. No decoding rings being available at the time, the next best thing was used – Italians. Cesare Bonesana di Beccaria is credited with introducing the Classical School of Criminology. "Crime and deviance is part of human nature", he argued, "and I will fucking punch your ticket if you disagree." Scholars did not kid around in the late 1700's. Just try reading his tome - <u>On Crimes and Punishment</u> – and see if you can find even a single pun or sarcastic jibe. Not going to happen. Not to be outdone, along came Cesare Lombroso in the late 1800's who stood on his hind legs and announced that the Positivist School of Criminology was the correct theory of crime and deviance. People were reo nato or "born criminals". Beccaria, he declared "Was a minor league Milanese thinker prone to bedwetting." A bona fide criminal is recognizable by his/her physique. Savage, knuckles rubbing the ground, and primal in behavior, much like an IRS tax auditor, these creatures were deviant because of biological / genetic inheritance. He labeled such people atavists. They were a short step or two from backsliding into the primal swamp of human evolution but made it to dry ground and a career as fitness coaches. Lombroso also believed that artistic genius e.g. Michelangelo, Mozart, and Walt Disney, was the product of inherited insanity, so take this guy with a large dose of commonsense. What Beccaria, Lombroso, and a few others did succeed in doing was kick open the flimsy door of conventional thought. Alternative views of what causes crime and deviance sprouted up in later decades; professors and practitioners woke up in time to apply for grants and write all sorts of theories about crime. Frankly, what any of them might say about a 51-year-old Florida lesbian who recently was accused of assaulting her lover with a dildo is arguable. Perhaps one or more of the following theories might help offer some insights.

<u>Demonology</u>; This one does not work so well for atheists. Its premise is that a criminal is possessed of mens rea (evil mind) because of a satanic presence. Known as a "last ditch" defense for defendants, it is enjoying a recent revival with numerous incidents of infanticide in which or both parents annihilated their children to spare the innocent from damnation or to purge said victim(s) from their state of "ungrace". Drowned, shoved in the microwave, flayed alive, tortured, burned, dismembered, strangled, destroyed as human beings by some extraordinarily inhuman parents. Do these actions even remotely sound like the acts of a mentally stable person, at least from the neck up? Therein lays the problem. Keep in mind with this theory that there are those who think evil is Satan. The defendant supports the idea that an evil entity – Satan, Hoodoo Sam, take your pick – exists and has occupied one's body or that of a child / family member. Being the compassionate sort, I would reply – "Fuck you. The only demon in this case is the killer." Fortunately, no defendant to my knowledge has succeeded in passing the chalice of righteous responsibility for diabolical acts unto the overworked, unappreciated, much maligned shoulders of Beelzeebub:

*"Zakieya Latrice Avery was charged with first-degree murder of her 1-and 2-year-old children plus two counts*

*of attempted murder of a 5-and an8-year-old girl. She stabbed two to death during an exorcism and tried to kill the other two children. A second woman, Monifa Denise Sanford, was also charged."*

Is there room in one body for more than one? But that is just me wondering why organized religions invariably need to blame some other entity when their members fuck up. The demonic theory is wonderfully useful for shifting blame to an ethereal, supernatural being who cannot be hauled into the docket to explain himself to the jury. Let's be fair. Doesn't Satan deserve an attorney?

<u>Free-Will Theory</u>; This is an extension of the Classical School of Crime. Jeremy Bentham is aptly credited with advancing this explanation. Moreover, this theory has enormous popularity within America. It gives a nifty one-two punch to explaining crime that has both intuitive and moral appeal. Mass shootings, burning of churches, road rage incidents, head-on car crashes with a drunk driver, animal abuse, in short – almost everything could have its roots in this theory. Free-will theory has four simple parts:

1. Everyone has the capacity for free will. We all get to choose what we do. Humans, by nature, seek out pleasure – "OMG! Is that a sushi bar?!!" and avoid pain (S&M fans step to the curb, please). We calculate each important decision using a formula. What are

the costs and benefits of my decisions? Consequences matter to the rational person and this theory is all about rational, objective decision making. No messy impulses or emotions for me, thank you ever so much. No unconscious motivators – "I slept with my twin sister's husband!" or irrational needs like attending a NASCAR race hoping some driver might crash into the safety fencing.

Since so many of us are self-centered, self-absorbed takers of endless selfies of babies, puppies, and places we visited, I think you can see why Bentham and his cronies devised a wickedly tidy theory of crime. Talk about sex appeal! A schematic for behavior that is all about me? What's not to like?

2.  To prevent crime government must provide deterrence sufficient to restrain us. As we slouch on the sofa and ponder our next rational decision it helps to know what the outcome and consequences of the act might be. Hmmm...if I put a 24/7 wiretap on every cell phone and computer in America I might get arrested for violating the 4th Amendment which protects people from unreasonable searches and seizures. Ooops! Sorry, National Security Agency, that was a cheap shot at your expense. Of course you are entitled, authorized, and expected to listen in on all of our digital transmissions. Sensitive, confidential, classified information is

open to your surveillance, which is as it should be. I am heartened (and oddly aroused) by the image of a Harvard or Stanford geek-graduate-employee of the NSA discreetly masturbating while eavesdropping in on a saucy conversation between two consenting adults. No, let's refocus. I buy a drone from WalMart with a GoPro Camera attached and fly it over a playground full of children. Ooops, my error again. Only the police and government are supposed to do that, for reasons that are unclear to me.

One last try – at a high school party the host parents donate a beer keg to the festivities. All of the attendees are underage. The deterrent effect is the prospect of being sued and arrested for being such stupid, careless parents. And for being allowed to breed. Only in this instance deterrence failed to prevent either the party or the parental breeding.

3. To succeed in deterring mom and dad from adding their mugshots to the family scrapbook, Bentham stated that the prospect of punishment is required. The pain of punishment must outweigh any anticipated pleasure from the deed by one degree or more. The rational side of us will respond by saying – "No, I shan't commit that act. It hurts more than it feels good." Like spending $200 a month to exercise at a fitness club and then getting a groin pull the first

week while lifting deadweights." The prospect of more pain is not worth the pleasure of ogling the babes in sweaty exercise shorts and sports bras. That leaves us with...

4.  ...the idea that effective punishments, the type that make us pause and reconsider, must be quick, certain and fairly applied. A swift slap to the head, for example, is an effective punishment. It certainly gets the undivided attention of the recipient.

Id, ego, and superego; This is Freudian theory. Think penis and vagina at war with one another or maybe being just playful? The id is where you go for counseling at $150. an hour. The ego is that piece of one's personality that always murmurs sweet somethings about you to yourself. Or, in my case, produces some delightful, one-sided arguments with myself. The superego is the tiny, tiny, almond slice of our brain that helps us ignore the effects of gravity upon our tits and ass. How does this theory explain crime? I think it has to something to do with having sex with grandma or grandpa? It is too complex (I have been waiting to dust off that pun) for me to explain.

Conflict Theory; This is one of my all-time favorites. Conflict theory is about inequality cued to the structure of our society. Mass marketing, media agendas, corporate maneuvers, government truth-speak, wage inequities, and a skewed political process that rewards candidates with multi-million dollar war chests as opposed to real talent, these are but a few items of conflict theory. Shrinking this theory to a simple example might help:

A newly minted college graduate emerges from the Ivory Halls of Wisdom at the University of Sameness with a degree in English Literature, the rough value equivalent of acquiring another hole in one's ass. Unless the diploma was acquired through an online school in which case the graduate will be selling plasma soon to pay down the tuition loans. The graduate, however, is confident and assured. She/he (transgenders welcome) wants an apartment, a job, some extra pocket money and at least a reasonable chance of success in life. After all, so conflict theory goes, we are bombarded from the womb with images and slogans and illusions of great jobs, even greater sex and endless happiness if we just "work hard". These same theorists argue that it is all a sham, a masquerade of falsehoods that most graduates will never, ever realize. Multiple that imaginary number of falsehoods times infinity which represents the realities of life choices available for everyone else. That does not sate the need by consumers for overpriced fashion shoes, a two-week vacation in Florida, and Botox injections.

It is not going to happen. This barbed-wire enema, the conflict scholars state, creates a person who no longer cares about consequences (adios Jeremy Bentham). This state of life creates dangerous people, sociopaths, psychopaths, suicidal and angst-ridden mindsets conducive to all types of crimes and acts of deviance. In short, no healthy society should tout the religion of celebrities and billionaires to a citizenry that cannot earn sustainable wages ($32,000) or find public transport to get to work. If you offer me the luxuries of life but deny me the means to achieve them I may snap and decide to take them from you. By force. Often and probably without remorse as I hurt you.

Conflict Theory is sometimes referred to as the Frankenstein Theory. We create the monster of have and have nots. No one should be surprised in the least if the have nots get organized (e.g. unions, equality of marriage rights, civil rights groups, urban rioting, etc.) and start demanding their fair share of the American Dream of unbounded happiness where double lattes, sushi bars, and designer handbags are as abundant as lemon drop candies.

In the interests of fairness and keeping the inventory to manageable size, I have assembled some crude interpretations for a few other theories of crime and deviance. Each has something revealing about why people commit crimes. Perhaps one or more may appeal to the reader.

Phrenology; measurement of the skull. The brain is the organ of the mind, so this theory goes, and by feeling the skull one can detect behaviors and functions of the person. In this case we map the skull (bumps, concave areas, horns) in order to identify the criminals. This is a fun but totally useless theory of crime.

Somatotypes (body types); people's character and behavior is determined / reflected in their body shape. Fatties (endomorphs), for example, are fun, easy going people. Santa Claus is fat. True criminals are muscular, energetic, and nervous, something along the lines of an Ethiopian marathon runner.

Anomie; The idea that someone does not "fit" the values of a society and who is only marginally interested in following its rules. This is a lost, disconnected individual or group that can be extremely dangerous (see socio and psychopath) under the right circumstances. Not to be confused with Bigfoot researchers, the New England Patriots, or environmentalists who attach solar panels to their roofs that melt the siding on their neighbor's homes.

Labeling; think self-fulfilling prophecy. Someone absorbs, integrates the terms and labels applied to him by others and acts upon them. It rarely applies to I.Q.'s, however, and is most often used to perpetrate the greatest single fraud unleashed on children, that they "can be anything they want to be." Hopefully none of them want to derail trains or shoot police but, alas, we know better. So stop telling your children this myth of disappointment. It only makes you feel better about yourself and gives the kid a false sense of hope. Be honest. That creepy kid who stares out of the classroom window all day? Forget the label of self-improvement and focus on crime prevention with that one.

I am omitting any discussion of other theories such as Deterrence, XYY chromosome, Biosocial Criminology,

Psychological, Operant Conditioning, Strain, Drift, Social Disorganization, Learning, Illegitimate Opportunity Structure, and the Psychoanalytic Approach, among many others, because frankly they are very boring and nowhere near as interesting as my hand crafted, razor sharp theory of crime. For the first and probably only time, I offer this succinct, incisive analysis as to why people commit crimes and how they justify doing so.

## The Cheesecake Theory of Crime

By
Dr. Daniel S. Campagna

This explanation, like many of my ideas in this book, is odd. I am reasonably familiar, over time, with all of the basic theories of crime and deviance and am dissatisfied with all of them for having too many leaks and too much brown water in the plumbing or "mental waterworks." The Cheesecake Theory (my copyright pending somewhere) of mine fixes all of those shortcomings.

The basic premise of the Cheesecake Theory is that people function according to a tripod of motivations broadly defined as Power, Pleasure, and Profit. A person's interpretation of one or more of these motivations may seem illogical to us but rational to him or, in this instance, to a female legislator:

*"Maryland State Delegate Ariana Kelly was charged with trespassing and indecent exposure in June after she*

75

*arrived at her ex-husband's home to drop off their kids and learned that his girlfriend was inside. According to police, she started banging on the door and ringing the bell repeatedly and, aware that her husband had a camera trained on the doorway, she faced it, exposed her breasts and shook them, one in each hand, toward the lens. Eventually, she dared an officer to arrest her. (The Washington Post reported that Kelly is a member of a legislative task force studying maternal mental health issues.")*

Washington Post, 7-14-2015

One's criminal and deviant needs, like Maslow's Hierarchy of basic needs, can be explained and easily understood (no modesty here) with my theory. To accomplish this please consider the following scenario.

You love cheesecake on a scale of yearning matched only by a Republicans' desire to avoid black people at parties and the desire of Democrats to apologize for them. At this particular party, there remains one very gorgeous slice of cheesecake left on a serving tray in the kitchen. You are alone and not very hungry but that piece of desert is beckoning to you. Eat me, it whispers. You crave that last slice more than sex, a new job and clean underwear. Before that happens, however, your inhibitions and common sense (1,500 calories per slice!), and logic must be overcome in a manner that is justifiable to the occasion (one's craving). We begin to spin the Tibetan prayer wheel of sacred excuses and rationalizations quickly, latching onto the one that makes us push aside our itchy discomforts and enables us to indulge our yearning.

The deed is done. As Oscar Wilde noted, "The only way to get rid of temptation is to yield to it." And thus our pleasure nodes are flooded with the creamy sensations of that delicious cheesecake. Now dispose of the incriminating evidence. Put the fork and plate in the sink and return to the party with your sorry ass cheesecake breath and flushed face. "Ah, 1,500 calories be damned! Tomorrow I shall diet."

Power, pleasure and profit are, in my opinion, the three most recurring themes of crime and deviance. The pursuit of one or more of these items helps explain much of what makes our society so lawless. Deciding to devour the slice of cheesecake, clearly, is the decision making process that flattens the psychological highways of doubts, fears, and anxiety and allows us to forge ahead with or without a clear conscience. Salving one's conscience so as to "feel" good about ourselves is almost irrelevant. The goal is to find a way to neutralize our innate objections and inhibitions and proceed to the act. In short, to justify something we should regret, like throwing underwear onstage at a Barry Manilow concert. Perhaps we all have a secret side to our identity that yearns for a chance to unleash our "other" self?

*"A jury in Atascadero, California, having already convicted Mark Andrews, 51, of murder, concluded in March*

*that he was legally sane at the time he shot his neighbor to death even though he claimed she was a vampire and that he himself had been, for 20 years, a werewolf."*
*KEYT-TV (Santa Barbara), 3-10-2015,*
*KPIX-TV (San Francisco, 4-9-2015*

Hopefully those other selves are creative, constructive personalities not Tasmanian Devils (or werewolves) looking for the next meal or those with psychological disorders, of which 61,500,000 Americans experience annually (1 in 4 adults). Besides, we tend to forget that a criminal act is not a one-dimensional thing; adults swap roles as offenders and victims throughout life.

# Criminal Defenses

Much like theories of crime, there is a wide array of excuses (defenses) available to a defendant. Anyone accused of a crime and routed into the judicial process by the filing of formal charges is expected, in most cases, to present some sort of explanation or defense for his behavior.

Q: Was it your intent Ms. Scarlet to kill Colonel Mustard in the Ballroom with a Candlestick?
A: No, your honor. It was my intent to ward off his sexual overtures by pushing him away.
Q: Yet you "pushed" him with a candlestick, allegedly, and ended up cracking open his skull and rendering him deceased. How do you explain that?

A: Your honor, I was terrified at the prospect of having sex with Colonel Mustard and may have used too much force out of fear.

Q: Why were you so terrified of a sexual encounter with Colonel Mustard?

A: He was a hermaphrodite, your honor.

Q: Oh. No further questions.

Defenses came in a wide spectrum of colors which is to say they range from seriously valid (legal duty to act) to seriously fucked up and desperate (alien abductions, transgender status, and sleepwalking homicides). The defendant hopes that an acceptable defense or explanation will result in a lesser charge (partial defense) / sentence or dismissal of the charges (full defense) as in the case of someone who uses force to legally defend himself from a home invasion. In either event, shrugging one's shoulder is a piss-poor defense as is "whatever". That is why lawyers were invented, to help us from falling on the sword of ignorance when confronted with criminal charges. Assuming we grasp the notion that sometimes we are not accountable for our misdeeds, let's consider some of the more traditional and a few avant-garde criminal defenses available to us.

- Insanity; "Your honor, I blame Elvis Pressley and his hip swinging music for my crimes." The insanity defense has several flavors and is very difficult to prove. The goal of this defense is to show that the defendant lacked the mental competency to understand that his acts were wrong and should not be held criminally liable. In most states the defendant must demonstrate insanity (burden of proof). It rarely succeeds, about 25% of the time and few (1% or so) of the felony cases in the United States involve an insanity defense. Sometimes known as the right from wrong test, in general, it is a last ditch defense unless one's client is 100% batshit, howls at the moon crazy and has a documented history of prior treatment for mental illness and very deviant conduct. This tends to contradict the fact, noted previously, that 61 million citizens annually suffer from some type of mental disorder. It would seem that this is one defense with real potential. Not anymore. Shoot up a theater, blow up a marathon race, gun down a school full of children, and see if an insanity defense will fly. Short answer – when society wants its bucket of blood from a defendant in revenge for a heinous act, few defenses on earth are likely to succeed. Perhaps, at a primal level, that is as it should be?

- Entrapment / Police Fraud; This occurs when the police entice someone to do something they would not ordinarily do. The police, in other words, set up the conditions for a crime e.g. operating a sting operation – call girl service and encourage and solicit the defendant to act on the lure or offer. If the court agrees with the defendant, it is an acquittal. The police are, in principle, not supposed to be in the business of pretending to be criminals; that sort of blurs the lines of right and wrong a bit. Moreover, there are enough police dedicated to unlawful behaviors (read=crooks) to make entrapment somewhat redundant.

- Intoxication / Impaired State; This is a familiar defense. The defendant is arguing for a partial mitigation or reduction in charges because he was under the influence of drugs and/or alcohol. The premise here is that one cannot completely form criminal or evil intent if you are looped or high. "Affluenza", on the other hand, is contrived defense that says rich young defendants do not understand their responsibilities because of the sheltered, entitled life provided for them by their indulgent parents. Sounds like an incredibly irresponsible, self-serving defense for rich juveniles? It is but it works in the state of Texas:

*Ethan Couch, 16-year-old from a rich family in Keller, Texas, drove a pickup truck while intoxicated (DWI) and killed four people. The judge believed that Couch did not deserve the full wrath of the law given his "illness" as an entitled douchebag.*

- Provocation; Not as popular a defense as it once was, the defendant claims that he was put into a state of "high distress" by circumstances and stimuli beyond his control and behaved in an atypical manner thus overriding his full liability for the crime. Failing a driver's road exam repeatedly, for instance, and ending with a crash into the examiner's car is a ready example of provocation.

- Hot Blood Defense; A defense that claims a defendant lost control of his reason momentarily due to a surfeit of emotions and thus acted out of character. Infidelity, being fired, harassment, and related events can churn up a whirlwind of negative emotions and reactions, among them homicide and assaults. The defendant is saying that he cannot account for his atypical behavior fully because he was in the grip of a violent, emotional urge to strike out, very similar to the experience of a tax audit or listening to advice from one's divorce attorney. Acting in the heat of the moment best sums up this defense.

My advice to future defendants? Be creative with your defense. Try this one – "A big boy done it and ran away." In other words, let your imagination guide you to a righteous acquittal or dismissal of all charges. And an apology from the court for wasting your time. Call me if that happens, by the way, and I will buy the first round to celebrate!

## Maxim

The Cheesecake Theory of Crime and Deviance is a reincarnated version of the idea we hold dear to our psyche. Bad things probably won't happen to me. If they do, the consequences will not be excessive. If they are, I will weather the storm as it is a one-time event. No lightning, in other words, strikes twice in the same spot. This sense of calculation involves denial, evasion, reassurance, and the hope that our crimes and deviant acts (shooting cats with pellet guns and peeping in the neighbor's bedroom window) are marginal enough to avoid public attention. What I firmly believe, however, is that everyone takes a bite of the cheesecake (even diabetics) when the need arises. Excessive speeding, cheating on an exam, lying to a police officer are simple demonstrations of the Cheesecake Theory. It works in most situations to explain how and sometimes why we commit crimes and deviant acts.

The process of locating a justification is merged with the inner need of wanting to do something we suspect may be unethical or legal. Enough self-interest, churning inside, moves us to the calculations (process) necessary to pull off the dirty deed. Feel bad today? Relax! Tomorrow there will be lots more cheesecake slices waiting for you. Apparently, as a species we have a genetic code or some sort of intuitive reflex that allows most of us to feel righteous about our crimes of person and property. We project our needs onto others. We weave elaborate explanations for errant behaviors e.g. speeding is okay to avoid being late for church, taking hotel towels ("they won't miss them"), and lying to your son's teacher about his missing homework ("he was sick."). In our own defense and to avoid any possibility of punishment we become the DaVinci's of criminal improvisation. Our genius for excusing ourselves while blaming others appears to be a bottomless pit of possibilities. I am not sure that is good news.

Looking Elsewhere
_Psychopathia Sexualis;_ Richard Freiherr von Krafft-Ebing, 1886

http://www.nij.gov/topics/corrections/recidivism/Pages/welcome.aspx

http://www.motherjones.com/kevin-drum/2014/12/broken-windows-broken-theory-crime

http://www.nij.gov/topics/corrections/recidivism/Pages/welcome.aspx

# Five

## SIR ROBERT PEEL AND AMERICAN POLICE

*"When you have police officers who abuse
citizens, you erode public confidence
in law enforcement. That makes the
job of good police officers unsafe."*

MARY FRANCES BERRY

For all practical purposes American law enforcement
began with the introduction of the Metropolitan Police
in London in 1829. Sir Robert Peel is credited with launching
the first formal police department in an industrialized nation.
Small and very different from any other peace keepers e.g.
night watch, this radical approach to keeping the peace arose
in response to a widespread breakdown of public order in the
greater London area. It was time when a handful of industri-
alists became the super-rich magnates of enormous influence

over trade, commerce, and government, legislation protecting machinery was put in place, people were imprisoned for causing damage to such machines, and children (bless their wee hearts) were forced to work 10-16 hours a day for a few pence in coal mines, assembly lines, slaughter pens, and funeral homes. Stop me if you have heard this story before.

Wide ranging capitalists exploited the legislative process (corrupting the House of Lords and Commons). The poor were used as EUE's (Expendable Units of Energy). Technology replaced the rule of law and organized religion preached the gospels of wealth and power. Schools drilled the notions of conformity, unquestioning obedience, and the "Queen and Country" themes into the skulls of children (middle and upper class only, sorry the poor get fucked here too). The accumulation of capital and assets skimmed from the staggering profits of wholesale exploitation of cultures and natural resources at home and in colonies continued without relief. Wars were constantly being fought against just about everyone who did not step in line with Britannia, and voila! a threshold was reached. That threshold involved the cries of "We can't take this shite anymore!!!" from the masses whose lives had as much practical value as shoestrings to the people in places of power and opportunity. It was a period in British history when gin cost less than food, when opium was readily available, prostitution rampant, high infant mortality rates, women used as objects to be discarded in pauper's graves, and short lives. Fuck Mary Poppins and the chimney sweeps. The entrepreneurs encouraged the use of small children to clean out the creosote in the chimney stacks.

Stopped me yet? What Sir Robert Peel and his cronies did was introduce the revolutionary notion of a professional police force to help maintain the public order (whatever shape that took). Nine Principles of Policing were issued to every new police officer or "Bobbie" as the public came to know them. These nine principles migrated to the United States where law enforcement in the 1800's resembled a collage of sheriffs, constables, volunteers (think= primitive community watch), and militia to help sweep up runaway slaves, deviants, and anyone else who did not march in time with the rest of white society.

If you have ever, and I hope you have, wondered what about the bedrock philosophy of American policing, look no further. These Nine Principles of Policing represent the goals, mission, and values of the first organized, professional police force. These principles, simply, put, inform us about the roles of law enforcement. Follow me as we do a brief comparison between these expectations of police behavior and their translation within the context of modern policing in America. Given the dysfunctional state of affairs with law enforcement throughout the nation, e.g. deadly car chases, police pepper spraying kneeling protestors, shooting unarmed people, breaking into the wrong homes with SWAT teams and flash bang grenades, Colorado Sheriffs refusing to enforce the laws regarding gun control, escalating a traffic stop from a citation to a beating by police, it seems appropriate to go back to our roots in 1829 to see where we have gone wrong in 2016.

# Peel's Nine Principles of Policing

1. To prevent crime and disorder, as an alternative to their repression by military force and severity of legal punishment.

Translation: No militarized cops need apply. The British public initially saw these newly minted officers as another extension of government force and suppression. The goal of American police is to protect all, prevent crime, and maintain order, not play G.I. Joe at our expense. Except -

> *"According to a* New York Times *(June, 2104) article at minimum, 93,763 machine guns, 180,718 magazine cartridges, hundreds of silencers and an unknown number of grenade launchers have been provided to state and local police departments since 2006. This is in addition to at least 533 planes and helicopters, and 432 MRAPs—9-foot high, 30-ton mine-resistant ambush protected armored vehicles with gun turrets and more than 44,900 pieces of night vision equipment, regularly used in nighttime raids in Afghanistan and Iraq."*

http://www.wsws.org/en/articles/2014/06/16/mipo-j16.html

# The Cheesecake Theory of Crime

Grenade launchers? MRAP's? Airplanes and helicopters? What offenders are those meant for? Here's what we get when the police own weapons and vehicles designed for the military:

> *"In 2010, a police SWAT team threw a stun grenade through the window of a Detroit home, setting fire to the blanket of seven-year-old Aiyana Jones, who was sleeping on a couch next to her grandmother. Seconds later, the SWAT team stormed through the door and shot Aiyana through the neck, killing her."*

http://theweek.com/speedreads/447874/interactive-map-paramilitary-police-raids-terrifying-depressing

2. To recognize always that the power of the police to fulfill their functions and duties is dependent on public approval of their existence, actions and behavior, and on their ability to secure and maintain public respect.

Translation: Respect by citizens for police (or anyone in positions of power) should not be automatically granted because someone wears a badge and has the lawful authority to: 1) kill us 2) arrest us (deprivation of rights) 3) beat us (within limits) 4) watch us (surveillance via the Patriot Act) and 5) place us into custody. Respect is earned. If you believe costumes (uniforms), a badge and other paraphernalia entitle anyone to be your boss, think again. We are afraid of police. Resentment and hatred are close companions of fear. I can recall my first experiences as a deputy sheriff/correctional officer (badly trained in both) walking among the public. The pale blue uniform, gold badge, .357 Smith & Wesson Model 19 revolver, handcuffs, and thick Sam Browne belt on my hip was distinctive and ominous to me. A constant reminder that my misjudgments could have serious consequences.

> *NEW YORK (AP) — "Officials in the nation's largest police department said Friday they uncovered dozens of instances of crimes misreported and wrongly downgraded by officers at a precinct after an anonymous tip to internal affairs and now 19 officers face departmental charges."*

*http://news.yahoo.com/19-ny-police-officers-face-charges-downgrading-crimes-011055340.html?nf=1*

3. To recognize always that to secure and maintain the respect and approval of the public means also the securing of the willing co-operation of the public in the task of securing observance of laws.

*"Robert Davis, a retired elementary school teacher from New Orleans, was arrested and brutally beaten by police on suspicion of public intoxication. On the night of Oct. 9, 2005, just a little over a month after Hurricane*

*Katrina, Davis returned to New Orleans to check on his family's property and went to the French Quarter to buy cigarettes. There, he was attacked by four police officers who said he was belligerent and resisted arrest by not allowing them to handcuff him. The beatings were videotaped by an Associated Press producer, who was also assaulted that night. The officers were either fired or suspended for their involvement, but many of the charges against them were cleared."*

*http://www.criminaljusticedegreesguide.com/features/10-worst-cases-of-police-brutality-in-history.html*

Translation: The New Orleans police department (and government) has a long history of corruption and deviance that has gone unchecked. A segment of that department consists of crooks wearing badges and uniforms. Notice that even the videotape producer in the above incident was attacked by the police. Peel was right. Society needs police to preserve order but the police need us to be cooperative. Nowhere in that simple message does it imply that the use of chokeholds, Tasers, and beatings by crooked cops is an automatic response to compel obedience.

4.  To recognize always that the extent to which the co-operation of the public can be secured diminishes proportionately the necessity of the use of physical force and compulsion for achieving police objectives.

Translation: Force, like power, can lose its effectiveness with over-use and abuse. Too much "overkill", so to speak, by the police gives the impression of corruption, indifference and poor self-control. The more citizens are injured by police, in other words, the more likely they are to eschew support for the local gendarmes. A community should not be beaten into compliance.

> *"In 2006, the home of 92-year-old Kathryn Johnston was raided on the basis of a fabricated tip. She did not realize the men entering her home were police officers, and she pulled a gun on them. The Atlanta police gunned her down."*

The Atlanta police gunned down a 92-year-old woman? My guess is that Ms. Johnston was terrified and pulled her gun. Based on the outcome she had a reason to be fearful.

> *"A Cleveland police officer who stood on the hood of a car and fired his gun 49 times through the windshield at two unarmed passengers was on Saturday found not guilty on two counts of voluntary manslaughter."*

A police officer was acquitted after shooting 49 bullets into a car at two unarmed passengers while standing on the hood of the car. Does anyone see this behavior as "askew", besides me? And finally,

> *"Said Dustin Theoharis, now 32, "Sometimes (police) make mistakes." Theoharis was napping in a friend's*

*house in Puyallup, Washington, when police arrived to arrest the friend's son, and when Theoharis reached for his ID, one officer imagined a gun, and the two officers opened fire (16 shots), hitting Theoharis in the jaw, both upper arms, both lower arms, wrist, hand, shoulder, abdomen and both legs. He spent months in a hospital and skilled nursing facility and today is largely immobile and unable to work. (He "won" legal settlements totaling $5.5 million, but one-third went to lawyers, and much of the rest has paid medical bills)."*

*Seattle Times, 3-21-2015*

Puyallup police shot an unarmed man in bed 16 times? That, my friends, does not encourage community support. Trust evaporates the more you abuse it. Peel and his cronies recognized that clear principle 186 years ago. The police are not supposed to be an occupying military force. They serve us, not the other way around. The above examples are the proverbial tip of the iceberg. Take a look at this site for more cases:

https://the7thpwr.wordpress.com/accidental-police-shootings/

5. To seek and preserve public favor, not by pandering to public opinion, but by constantly demonstrating absolutely impartial service to law, in complete independence of policy, and without regard to the justice or injustice of the substance of individual laws, by

ready offering of individual service and friendship
to all members of the public without regard to their
wealth or social standing, by ready exercise of cour-
tesy and friendly good humor, and by ready offering
of individual sacrifice in protecting and preserving
life.

*"A gay, female police officer in Bogota, New Jersey lost
her job for protecting a suspect from a beating by other
officers. She was later reinstated. The official reports
filed about this incident reveal lies made by the Chief of
Police and attacking officers"*

http://news.yahoo.com/video/officer-fired-stopping-beating-
gets-193103026.html

This type of story should have been banner media headlines
everywhere – a police officer protected a suspect. What was
the official response of those in charge of the Bogota Police
Department? Fire the gay officer for dereliction of duty. For
the record, the officer was eventually reinstated.

Translation: For absurdity's sake, even 186 years ago it was
recognized that the police departments had to be composed
of people (men for starters) who were not alpha, high testos-
terone John Wayne/Dirty Harry caricatures living out some
screen fantasy of "catching the scumbags! Aside from the fact
that police are lousy shots and most officers will never draw

and fire their weapons, there is still a sense of "man overboard" mentality with these various incidents.

http://www.washingtonpost.com/sf/investigative/2015/04/11/thousands-dead-few-prosecuted/

6. To use physical force only when the exercise of persuasion, advice and warning is found to be insufficient to obtain public co-operation to an extent necessary to secure observance of law or to restore order, and to use only the minimum degree of physical force which is necessary on any particular occasion for achieving a police objective."

*"Chicago police officer Marco Proano allegedly shot over a dozen bullets at a moving car with six underage black occupants. None of the occupants had a weapon or had threatened the officer. Two passengers were hit by the bullets."*

http://www.businessinsider.com/chicago-police-officer-taped-opening-fire-on-a-car-full-of-black-teens-2015-6

Chicago officer Proano has some explaining to do, unless it is his habit to shoot first then justify the act later. No threats, no guns, and yet he fired a dozen shots at a moving car.

Translation: We get it. Sometimes physical and deadly force is justified; it is the nature of the circumstances into which officers are sometimes placed. BUT – Peel argued that discretion is the better part of valor and there is no substitute for common sense and sound judgement. A sense of proportion to circumstances is helpful rather than a pre-conditioned response. That is not to say, however, that police work is always predictable. And I am fully aware of being an armchair general with some of these observations. The problem is that the extreme, chronic nature of these activities makes me challenge the usefulness of the vetting process that lead to the hiring of these officers. Overreactions goaded by hurried judgements and excessive force seem to characterize many of these cases.

7. *To maintain at all times a relationship with the public that gives reality to the historic tradition that the police are the public and that the public are the police, the police being only members of the public who are paid to give full-time attention to duties which are incumbent on every citizen in the interests of community welfare and existence.*

Translation: This is a brilliant principle. Consider its poignancy. Police are citizens (us). The myths of policing place a distance between the police and citizens and can erode the notion of police professionalism and mutual trust. Citizens volunteer to apply for the job of policing, no compulsion needed, and eventually they must put down the baton, so to speak, and return to the society from which they sprung. Or, in the words of Raymond Chandler;

*"Police business is a hell of a problem. It's a good deal like politics. It asks for the highest type of men, and there's nothing in it to attract the highest type of men. So we have to work with what we get..." (The Lady in the Lake)*

Here is a practical example of Chandler's observation.

*"Seven San Francisco police officers accused of sending racist and homophobic text messages have been suspended, and the police chief has recommended that they be fired."*

http://news.yahoo.com/3-san-francisco-officers-face-suspensions-over-racist-61326414.html

In all probability, these officers will not be fired but simply reassigned until the media and the public has lost interest in the case. Hopefully their next round of text messages will be less volatile?

8. *To recognize always the need for strict adherence to police-executive functions, and to refrain from even seeming to usurp the powers of the judiciary of avenging individuals or the State, and of authoritatively judging guilt and punishing the guilty.*

Translation: The closing part is a juicy bit. Police are not supposed to be judge and jury but they can easily be viewed as both. Peel was stating, it seems, the obvious; law enforcement has a specific set of functions that preclude acting as "avenging angels" and overstepping their lawful mandate to enforce the laws. They are legally obligated and bound by their oath of office to enforce all laws of their state or federal government. In other words, police must not put themselves in the role of judge (and jury). That condition is known as acting outside the letter of the law or in legal terms – acting like a Grade-A dickhead.  Is that not right you fifty-five Colorado sheriffs who have refused to enforce the new state gun laws? Hey! I have an idea. How about I refuse to obey your orders? You know, pick and choose the ones I like, right? If the police refuse to obey a court order or to enforce controversial laws, who can I complain to for help? Apparently this practice of serving as judge and cop is not uncommon:

> *"Ignoring a court order, police in Carrollton, Kentucky town put mentally ill man on bus to Florida."*

http://www.kentucky.com/2015/05/29/3874508_ignoring-court-order-police-in.html?rh=1

9. To recognize always that the test of police efficiency is the absence of crime and disorder, and not the visible evidence of police action in dealing with them.

Translation: Perception drives reality. If the public feels safe, they endorse their police. Of course, as noted in previous chapters, the American investment in all things criminal, from watching bait car arrests on television to making illegal wagers, means the police must routinely use discretion in determining whom to arrest (if at all) and for what. As for "visible evidence of police action", Peel had no way of predicting the advent of video recordings:

> *"Police body camera footage published online by a rights group on Thursday showed two (Barstow) California officers wrestling to the ground a black woman who was eight months pregnant, and arresting her following a dispute with another woman."*

http://news.yahoo.com/video-shows-california-police-wrestle-pregnant-black-woman-045331631.html

Hey Barstow P.D.!! – How many officers does it take to subdue an eight-month pregnant woman who is not resisting arrest?" Answer: Two because near-term pregnant woman have been known to sprint at speeds exceeding a barefoot waddle. "Bill! Grab her ankles, the perp might break her water and try to escape! " Frankly, my perception of public safety does not include the image of police tackling pregnant women. Teenagers, yes, because those hormonal creatures are both annoying and "like, OMG! like…"self-absorbed golems. But, otherwise, we may safely assume that Principle 9 is broken often and in many jurisdictions, such as the sleepy town of King City, California:

*" Residents of a California farming town (King City) were grappling Wednesday with the feeling that their trust has been violated after learning the acting police chief and a handful of officers were charged with crimes including selling or giving away the impounded cars of poor Hispanic residents (many of whom spoke no English)."*

http://news.yahoo.com/california-town-shaken-police-officers-arrested-235107533.html

# Questionable Practices of Police

If Peel's Principles are correct it is clear that American police would benefit greatly from abandoning questionable, often-times illegal and shady practices in the course of their daily work. It is beyond the scope of this guidebook to examine all of these practices in depth so I will offer a few of the more insidious, illegal practices happening today. Specifically, let us briefly consider civil forfeiture and asset seizures, hot pursuits, and corruption as examples of such practices.

# Civil Forfeitures

This involves the seizure of someone's cash and assets directly and immediately by police on the premise that it has some relationship to a criminal activity. For instance, if a nephew borrows your car to drive to a store and completes a purchase of marijuana from a local dealer, your car can be seized as an instrument of the crime, even though you had no knowledge of the nephew's intent. Expand this concept to include traffic stops and the taking of all the money a driver has in his/her possession. The officer can use the excuse that "you shouldn't have so much money with you." Sounds ludicrous? The driver typically has to sue the court in the jurisdiction where the money was stolen, eh, excuse me, seized by the officer in the vague hope of getting "some" of his money returned e.g. twenty cents on the dollar before lawyer's fees.

Although U.S. Attorney General Eric Holder recently banned the practice of asset seizure by local police, it continues to this day. Every year hundreds of millions of dollars, possibly a billion dollars or more, are "liberated" from drivers, preferably from those with out-of-state license plates, by police and transferred to their department and city budgets. It makes the police look like tax collectors and thieves, not a pleasant image. The practice of "stop and seize" is controversial and a violation of the basic right known as the presumption of innocence. Unfortunately, this practice of seizing of cash and property without sufficient justification happens routinely in every state. It thrives, in part, as the Washington Post pointed out in a lengthy investigation, with a little help from private industry:

"A thriving subculture of road officers on the network now competes to see who can seize the most cash and contraband, describing their exploits in the network's chat rooms and sharing "trophy shots" of money and drugs. Some police advocate highway interdiction as a way of raising revenue for cash-strapped municipalities."

http://www.washingtonpost.com/sf/investigative/2014/09/06/stop-and-seize/

Highway interdiction or, as I prefer to call it – highway robbery and shakedowns – by police departments is aided and abetted by private training firms that teach the best methods for "liberating" cash and assets from citizens. One such firm - Black Asphalt Electronic Networking & Notification System whose motto -"post your seizures, further your case" (only registered police departments may access the site) at https://bales.org/ shows police how to record and share confidential information about motorists on a nationwide basis. You know, sort of a Facebook for thieves with bragging rights in chat rooms for those officers who have taken the most cash and seized the most assets. You may think this practice and my comments are exaggerations; I urge you to rethink that by doing a simple topic search – police stop and search incidents or asset seizure practices. Decide for yourself. Nothing about this practice of civil forfeitures and asset seizures is commendable except in those cases where significant drug trafficking is clearly linked to the official taking of the profits and instruments (cars, homes, etc.) from the crime. But to swoop down and pick the pockets of drivers for cash? Maybe it's time to invite those departments to stop by and vacuum my sofa for spare change?

It is a corruptive practice without justification and puts the financial interests of government budgets ahead of the constitutional rights of its citizens. Think of it as you being victimized without cause or proof or even the bare bones of due process. And good luck with the lawsuit to recover your money, assuming you have any leftover cash to file a claim and the resources to pursue it. This is a cash cow that is welcome by many departments in criminal justice, usually at the (literally) expense of the poor and disenfranchised. In Oklahoma, for instance, an assistant District Attorney used (but later returned) seized cash to pay off his student college loans. If, by the way, you hear the argument that civil forfeiture and assets seizure are key pieces in the war against drugs, I recommend you examine the following site:

http://dailycaller.com/2015/01/30/the-7-most-egregious-examples-of-civil-asset-forfeiture/

# Hot Pursuits

The logic behind this questionable practice is simple - necessity. Sometimes fleeing suspects pose a grave danger to others e.g. drunk driver, certain types of felon. The decision to pursue requires the highest possible justification. Fleeing from a traffic citation is not a reason to chase. All hot pursuits are potentially high risk endeavors where things can spiral quickly out of an officer's control. A high speed chase is supposed to be a very calculated gamble, much like the rational choice theory. We weigh the costs and benefits before deciding what to do. This is a logical, orderly, and completely unlike reality because too often civilian casualties happen and millions of dollars in property damage accrue. In other words, much greater harm is caused in an attempt to prevent a lesser harm (catch the escapee). This is very bad on many levels.

Civilian casualties are labeled as unfortunate collateral damage. If you, as a police officer, believe this philosophy then let us first arrange for someone in your family to be killed or injured during a hot pursuit, as a sincere demonstration of your commitment to the logic. Sacrificing someone you do not know is irresponsible, terrible policy. Put someone you love on the wheel of life's misfortunes with a hot pursuit and let's see how devoted you are to this practice of hot pursuits. There is a level of hypocrisy in a policy that places blameless citizens at risk of death or injury in the interests of conducting a hot pursuit. The lives of those civilians matter more, in my opinion, than the policy justification for hot pursuits (with a few clear and evident exceptions). Ironically, sometimes (not often enough) the pursuit may be vital to the safety of others and addressed on a case by case basis. Yet the numbers involving injuries and fatalities suggest otherwise.

About 360 people are killed each year in police chases, according to the National Highway Traffic Safety Administration (NHTSA). The number of injuries is estimated to be in the thousands but reliable data is outdated and confined to a "need to know" basis by reporting police departments. NHTSA data is the closest thing available for weeding out the numbers of deaths and injuries resulting from hot pursuits. This sort of information need not be so cloaked in secrecy by police departments. Each department, by the way, is allowed to design its own policy regarding hot pursuits.

http://www,theiacp.org/Portals/0/pdfs/Publications/Police%20Pursuit.pdf

The decision to initiate a pursuit is akin to Russian Roulette, never quite knowing how it will turn out once the sirens are turned on. Here is what I think happens when a hot pursuit is initiated. The fleeing driver and officer go into an adrenaline overload. Time and vision is compressed and the five sense are altered by the laws of physics; sounds, images, stimuli are all distorted by the acceleration of man and machine within the auto(s). Judgment is affected. Add to this volatile mix an environment with civilians whose locations and movements add a terrible randomness to the pursuit. They may and do appear suddenly, unaware that a pursuit is in motion. Accidents and fatalities occur. The chase has very few end-game options: safe capture, injuries, death, property damage, and the rare escape. BUT – hot pursuits have become the stuff of media ratings:

http://www.bbc.com/news/magazine-31387485
(Why America Loves a Police Car Chase)

Apparently televised hot pursuits rank up there with Viagra, reality shows about rednecks who sell duck callers and stories about Siamese twins for freakish popularity with the networks.

Throw in a hijacked school bus, media helicopter crashes, a desperate man blowing his brains out on camera, and multi-car crashes on interstates and we have a spike in audience ratings! Think of police car chases as the modern day equivalent of the games in the Roman Coliseum The public sits in a semi-delusional trance aroused by the scenes of carnage and the prospect of imminent death (provided it is someone else). It is difficult to fault police trying to perform a necessary hot pursuit when it is transformed into a media circus event with the networks fighting for access to the ongoing drama.

## Corruption

Before opening up this Pandora's Box of bipolar, schizophrenic public angst about whether or not corruption is alive and thriving in law enforcement, let me offer a few facts to frame the discussion. Corruption within law enforcement in America has a long, complex and repetitive history of documented abuses and practices dating back to the 1800's. There was NEVER a time when law enforcement was pure and perfect, so to speak. That is a myth, like the image of an All-American family without dysfunctions.

> I'm a black ex-cop, and this is the real truth about race and policing;
> Redditt Hudson, May 28, 2015

http://www.vox.com/2015/5/28/8661977/race-police-officer

# The Cheesecake Theory of Crime

That's okay. Those myths need to go away, far away. The prairies of North Dakota are a good start. Reality is honest and we can work with it. Some police, just as we find in other professions, will falter and fail in the execution of their official duties through negligence and other corrupting habits. I am not referring to accepting minor gratuities e.g. free coffee at a convenience store but those habits and behaviors which violate the oath to protect and serve. The bulk of police work still involves calls for social service, serving court papers, traffic duty, but not "crime fighting". A modern police department is organized to handle those things predictably well. When officers begin to mistake their authority for license to abuse, the waters of corruption become very murky and full of hungry alligators with guns and badges. Numerous incidents have been included thus far that demonstrate when the police act illegally nothing much good comes of it for the citizenry. The list of such incidents is depressingly long and familiar. Thanks to the advent of video recorders in phones and handheld devices, these incidents quickly become news stories broadcast across the web. Excessive force, perjury, extortion, bribery, arrest without cause, lying on criminal complaints, coerced confessions, and drug trafficking are a few of the more prominent acts of corruption in law enforcement. They have been thoroughly documented in research since the 1950's. Still, there are plenty of officers with a hand in the till of corruption in some form.

What I am interested in are those explanations of police corruption and deviance. There is one such explanation that is chronically abused and trotted out routinely by departments and apologists for law enforcement. I am referring to the "always a few bad apples in the barrel" response to charges of police corruption. That explanation is another myth of criminal justice. It is a humdinger of a piss poor description for illegal conduct by people carrying a gun and wearing a badge. Let us consider a few contradictions of the rotten apple theory:

- How did the apples (police) get rotten (corrupted)?
- Is it possible the whole barrel (police department) is rotten? If so, how did it become rotten?
- How many apples does it take before we drop the "few" and get to "many?"
- Is this explanation a convenient way to minimize the harm of rotten apples by not addressing the cause of the spoilage?
- How do we get rid of a barrel that produces rotten apples and replace it with some other, healthier container?

Perhaps the answer, in part, is that a few apples can quickly spoil the whole barrel. Or maybe the whole barrel (police department) was rotten to begin with and no one noticed or cared? Is it not easier to blame a few?

Or is police corruption a matter of racial profiling, as some critics have claimed? We all live and embrace, to some degree, various types of racial and sexual stereotypes. Some of these stereotypes are quite flattering and have some basis in reality. The others, well, not so complimentary and not so linked to reality. But they exist and thrive nonetheless. Young black males wearing hoodies and reflective sunglasses (even at night when the sun is rarely out) raise the hackles and fears of white people. Yes, that is a generalization but I argue that it is a symptom of victimization, the sense that a wrong step or comment will elicit an immediate confrontation from these young men. The media promotes white fear of black crime; stories of young mothers going to their children's schools and beating up teachers and bus drivers, stories of flash mobs crashing into and looting retails stores, and the all too frequent news flash about the latest shooting fatalities in Chicago predominantly by black males (1,560 victims as of July 30, 2015 and on track to exceed the total rate for 2014 of 2,589 victims). This is a situation aggravated by too many variables beyond measure. What is abundantly clear (to me) is that police corruption is at least instigated by the popular belief that black males are more likely than not to commit crimes or acts of deviance. That's not fair but it is a candid view of what drives corruption, in part, and police response to black suspects real or imagined. What our society does to correct that impression is open to debate so start talking folks because this issue is not going away anytime soon.

## Maxim

I have devoted a rather lengthy, lopsided sermon on policing in America for one key reason. The police are the gatekeepers of the criminal justice system. They are the bottom-tier of the law enforcement hierarchy who exercise maximum discretionary power. They decide who is arrested or released, and what charges, if any, will be filed. It matters a great deal how these people define and perform their duties on a daily basis. In my opinion, the police are the single most important entity in the criminal justice system; without their input and decisions, nothing happens in the judicial process. There is, in short, so much at stake with law enforcement and resolving the problems that confront it. We are back, figuratively speaking, to the idea of myths and their value in criminal justice.

The myths surrounding law enforcement are tentacles that ensnare the unwary. Worse, too many departments believe those myths and try to fulfill them as self-serving prophecies about their roles in society. I fully acknowledge the fact that police must assume many roles; protector, social worker, social service provider, and trauma manager, to name a few. I also "get it"; police normally interact with citizens when we are in need (victims) or when we are the "bad guys." I have known a countless number of offenders over the last 35 decades of all shapes and sizes. Many of them were fearful, maniacal narcissists e.g. gangbangers, child pornographers, killers, and violent drug addicts. Some were deeply delusional and a few were just inept and more stupid than a convention hall full of neo-Nazis hosting another wet tee-shirt contest. The majority of offenders apprehended by police and processed in the courts are, as cited earlier, fairly mundane criminals with behavior patterns that are very familiar to veteran police officers. Those are the clientele whose problems and needs, often in stages of high trauma or completely out of control mindsets, intersect with law enforcement. In short, police routinely see us at our worst... It is no wonder, as a buffer from despair and chronic depression that police use crude humor, stereotypes, and generalizations about "us" in order to stay afloat in their work.

In the end Sir Robert Peel had it right. We have strayed from the universal values of protect and serve that are the Nine Principles of Policing. Those principles are as relevant today as they were for metropolitan London in 1829. It is time to reintegrate and restore all of them into American policing, from the local to state to federal jurisdictions. The rotten apple theory, by the way, is a load of manure dumped on our lawns by police departments who do a fairly poor job of supervising their employees. Certainly our capacity for corruption within criminal justice seems "persistent" to say the least, and we are collectively doing next to nothing to change that condition. Internal Affairs Unit and civilian review boards are normally overwhelmed by cases and often not given any true authority to resolve charges of corruption. Any hope for meaningful reform is going to happen elsewhere and probably in a very different manner:

Looking Elsewhere
http://nation.time.com/2013/09/16/ready-fire-aim-the-science-behind-police-shooting-bystanders/http://news.yahoo.com/city-blacks-nearly-9-times-more-likely-arrested-212814242.html

http://www.bloomberg.com/graphics/2015-doj-and-police-violence/

http://www.freep.com/story/news/local/michigan/2015/02/22/civil-asset-forfeiture-michigan-seizures-aclu-heritage-foundation-institute-justice/23737663/?utm_source=feedblitz&utm_medium=FeedBlitzRss&utm_campaign=usatoday-newstopstories

http://www.theiacp.org/Portals/0/pdfs/Publications/Police%20Pursuit.pdf

http://www.flatlandkc.org/news/pursuit/

http://www2.law.mercer.edu/lawreview/getfile.cfm?file=572031.pdfhttp://www.politico.com/magazine/story/2014/10/the-police-are-still-out-of-control-112160.html#.VbqPkynbKM9

http://www.justice.gov/sites/default/files/opa/press-releases/attachments/2015/03/04/ferguson_police_department_report.pdf

http://www.justice.gov/sites/default/files/opa/press-releases/
attachments/2015/03/04/ferguson_police_department_
report.pdf

# Six

ASS KICKING IN THE COURTS OF JUSTICE

*At the height of a political corruption trial, the prosecuting attorney attacked a witness. "Isn't it true," he bellowed, "that you accepted five thousand dollars to compromise this case?"*

*The witness stared out the window, as though he hadn't heard the question.*

*"Isn't it true that you accepted five thousand dollars to compromise this case?" the lawyer repeated.*

*The witness still did not respond.*

*Finally, the judge leaned over and said, "Sir, please answer the question."*

*"Oh," the startled witness said, "I thought he was talking to you."*

# The Cheesecake Theory of Crime

Mountains of studies have been conducted in the last 75 years about the judicial system, particularly the courtroom work group and how its functions (or not). That group's membership includes the Tier 1, three big league players – judge, prosecutor and defense attorney. Tier 2 consists of the bailiff (order in the court), clerk (docket and case files), court reporter (record of case), victim(s), witnesses (expert and lay), jurors (trials are infrequent) and the sad sack defendant. Notice I put the defendant last in this roster of "teammates."

This work group is noteworthy for its dynamics and expectations. Unlike other jobs where power is relative, if it exists at all below the level of management, the courtroom work group is a very select cadre of people who wield the "mighty sword of justice" on a daily basis in local, state and federal courtrooms throughout the country. Only two players in the cast of characters have real power. The judge especially and the prosecutor mostly delegate outcomes to an unending stream of criminal complaints. Most criminal cases are resolved via a negotiated settlement or plea deal to lesser charges, fewer counts. The defendant agrees to plead guilty in exchange for a reduced sentence. An estimated 90% of the criminal case dockets in the United States are concluded through a plea deal. Which means that:

- Criminal trials are uncommon. The notion of innocent until proven guilty is pabulum. Most defendants are either guilty, bullied into agreeing to a deal, terrified at the prospect of a full-blown sentence (if convicted, which odds are he will be), or steadfastly determined to prove their innocence (and likely to lose). If ever you are ordered to appear for possible service on a jury, do so. It is an interesting experience to sit with others during the voir dire process (screening of potential jurors) and watch how the well-oiled wheels of justice turn with the courtroom work group. I served as a foreman on a jury during a de novo trial. De novo means fresh but think of it as a "do over." The defendant used the not so famous "big black dog ran in front of her car" defense, causing her to crash at a high speed and wrap the engine block around a chain link fencepost. Actually, as was determined, the defendant had crashed after leaving her lover's residence in order to hurry home to her husband. The jury deliberated for at least 15 minutes. Guilty. The defendant argued with the judge and was cited for contempt (jail time). My memory of the case is that of a work group either irritated at the waste of time and cost for this second, frivolous trial or amused at the audacity of the defendant's conduct. The event was made more amusing by the fact that the defendant's husband sat glaring at her during the trial.

- A 90% plea deal rate means the work group agrees to resolve "similarly situated" cases the same way most times. The faces and names of the defendants change but not the crime. If there are no exceptional or mitigating factors to evaluate then why waste time with a trial? That makes a great deal of sense from the perspective of efficiency and using limited resources well.

- What is in the best interests of the defendant is not necessarily the plea deal. However, much like a car salesperson trying to make a pitch, the relevant members of the work group will do their utmost to persuade, threaten, cajole, and otherwise browbeat the defendant into a plea deal. "Besides, the group has seen 50 burglaries this month and you, Mr. Defendant, are simply the 51$^{st}$. We are offering you a great deal. Plead guilty and go home today." Then again, with a repeat offender, the plea deal is terra firma, a familiar place to coax a reasonable deal from the prosecutor.

- There is a penalty doled out to the accused for wasting a court's time if the verdict is guilty (it usually is). No matter that the defendant may think he is innocent or that a trial by jury or judge is a core right of our society, to a judge and prosecutor a guilty verdict means – "You did it. You knew you were guilty and you were hoping to wriggle out of the charge(s)." Maximum penalties for not pleading guilty but opting for trial are not uncommon.

- The judicial process is a rigged game in which the only constants are plea bargains, familiar faces and crimes in the courtroom, poor defendants, and pre-ordained outcomes. It is game of five-card stud poker but the defendant only gets two cards. Make them count.

We are conditioned to believe that a courtroom is a sacred place that something profound and vital to the wellbeing of society occurs in that place. All observers must keep silent and pay attention. Hats removed and no distractions introduced e.g. gum chewing, phones, etc. In this holy place, moreover, the judge is God (Quisnam praesumo meddle me! - Who Dares Meddle With Me!) and the super powers at his disposal rival those of comic book heroes. Fines, life sentences, findings of guilt or innocence (bench trial), contempt of court with immediate jail time, verbal admonishments, and sometimes they are even allowed to throw eggs at the defendant. In the courtroom the judge is the first and final word on everything that happens during the processing of a case. Outside the courthouse, at the grocery store or tennis court, the judge is just, well, just another swinging dick with zero authority over us. The same is true for prosecutors.

Keep in mind that the members of the courtroom work group are very familiar to one another. They learn how to accommodate the personalities and values of one another in order to keep the assembly line of cases moving to resolution. Plea deals are the lubricants that grease the wheels of that machine and keep things humming along, everything swell, and everyone content, aside from the defendant. Also, it does help to remember that if the right to a speedy trial was exercised in about 20% more cases, the backlog in courts would be stupendous (mathematical term meaning greater than "awful lot"). Society has neither the money nor resources to handle the overload.

What a pleasant "aren't we pretty darn swell people" feeling that must be. Dispense justice routinely because most cases are routine. The prosecutor and defense attorney sometimes spend a solid ten minutes debating the future of a defendant before announcing to the judge that a deal has been made. The judge will ask each defendant if he/she understand the terms of the deal. The defendant's role is simple – say "yes" or "no" to the offered plea bargain. A sentence is handed out. Case closed. Next! Did I say ten minutes? I meant to say five.

This myth of a neutral fact-finding process is a sham. Prosecutors need convictions to keep their jobs. Everyone in that work group has expectations of cooperation that can and often do run contrary to the best interests (and rights) of the accused. Of course there are plenty of defendants versed in plea negotiations. We call these people repeat offenders or "life's little losers" and they know that most crimes can be settled directly and with limited hassle. It is worth noting that the physical design and rules of the courtroom contribute to the sense of majesty and power needed to intimidate bystanders, defendants, and witnesses. The judges' dais, for instance, is elevated so as to distance the bench from everyone else (look down upon us Lord). The courtroom is rife with symbols and rituals, such as flags, law books, black robes of a judge, his gavel, jury box, subdued lighting and furniture, "All rise!", "Silence in the court!", etc. The only thing missing is <u>Bach: Jesu, Joy of Man's Desiring</u>, being softly piped in through ceiling speakers as background noise. The sense that something profound and darn important is happening in the room is amplified by the language of the group, the process of adjudicating (resolving) a case, and the realization that no one had better screw with the judge. His instructions are backed by the full faith and power of the state.

Let's toss these myths and symbols into the hamper for now and consider some other facts about the judicial process and the courtroom work group. There is much to recommend about the typical judicial process; it is predictable, organized, often logical, and able to produce a finished product – verdict and/or sentence – with reasonable dispatch when circumstances dictate. That is the good news but this is the flip side of that coin:

- A percentage of people who accept plea bargains but are technically innocent do so because they cannot abide waiting in jail or do not really understand the implications for pleading guilty. A mother accused of stealing from a big box retail store, for instance, will plead quickly to any light charges in order to return home to her children.
- These same people are indigent; too poor to afford the smallest cash bond needed to stay out of jail. The only "Get Out of Jail Card" they have to play is a

plea bargain; otherwise, the waiting room time to a trial may last more than a year. If/when acquitted of charges, the defendant will have lost his job, friends, income, and so forth. There is a popular notion among courtroom work groups that sometimes it is better that an innocent person be found guilty than a guilty person ever be freed. Which is okay provided you are not the innocent person being offered as the sacrificial lamb, so to speak. This is a recurrent theme in criminal justice.

- Power corrupts. Judges can extort compliance from attorneys by stalling a case and sticking it through a cycle of calendar calls that never lead to resolution. That is known as punishing an uncooperative defense attorney for wasting the court's time with numerous motions and filings on behalf of his client. Remember the idea of similar cases? The work group does not tolerate defense attorneys trying to level the playing field at the expense of court time and taxpayer money. No million dollar defenses, please.

- A key step in assuring transparency between the prosecutor and defense is known as discovery. Discovery is a simple step whereby both sides are supposed to "empty the bag" of all their evidence. No surprise witnesses, no misplaced DNA evidence, just a full and cooperative exchange of information. This is an uncommon event. The goal of the prosecutor is to win. Often. Discovery is not a mutually beneficial step. Prosecutors often "forget" or hide information from the defense attorney at discovery.

- As Grisham (below) and others have noted, sloppy police practices and faulty crime lab evaluations (that happens more often than you might think) produce false positive information. That is, such cases are built on tainted and false scientific evidence. Add to that condition the fact that eyewitnesses make for lousy, unreliable witnesses.

- People lie in the courtroom. Witnesses, victims, defendants, attorneys, police – from time to time they lie or "shade the truth" while acting out of necessity and one's best interests. Like needing to win a high profile case e.g. Duke Lacrosse rape case or to cover up falsified official police reports.

- Not all courtroom actors are created equal. Do not be fooled or impressed by the garb, demeanor, or title of anyone within a courtroom. Those things tell us nothing about the values and skills of the person. How prepared, for instance, are you to evaluate the ability of your attorney? What is that evaluation based on – appearance, poise, the gibber jabber of legalese, outcomes? Do any of us ever ask our lawyer, dentist, or doctor where he/she ranked in their respective graduating class at school? Clearly those people are not going to offer that information online or post it in their office. If he/she was not near the top 10% of the class then statistically and logically they are second or third best. Do you know where to look for records of complaints filed against an attorney? How many people do you know who can provide a referral on a competent defense attorney?

- The poor defendants get public defenders. These attorneys are often overworked, underpaid, operating with slim resources and spend one hour or two, if that much, with each client who they must persuade to accept a plea deal. Everyone else will spend thousands of dollars for the services of a private attorney. We earnestly hope he/she knows how to succeed with the courtroom work group. Good luck with that decision. Law schools devote few course hours in their curriculums to the topic of criminal defense work and procedures (no money to be made in that line of work). Purchase a lottery ticket afterwards, which is almost about the same odds of success as finding a competent private defense attorney. Criminal defense attorneys have a low status in courtrooms comparable to the custodians at interstate rest areas. Necessary, tolerated, but you would rather they dressed better. You will often find the private defense attorneys cruising the halls outside the courtrooms, drumming up business. Bring some cash, about $500, to secure their services. And if you hear an attorney in court request a continuance because "Mr. Green is absent" that means the defendant has not fully paid the counsel.

- The irony is that experienced defendants already know what to do, say, and expect. On more than one occasion, while waiting in the halls of a municipal courthouse, I have overheard defendants swap very precise information about judges and likely penalties for their cases.

- Judges and prosecutors make mistakes. Sometimes they even distort their positions of power and authority to reach an unjustified or illegal ends. Unseating or impeaching a judge or prosecutor, by the way, is a costly, rare event unless the actor behaves in a way so outrageous over a number of years that something must be done:

*"Pennsylvania Judge (Mark Ciavarella) Gets 'Life Sentence' For Prison Kickback Scheme"*
http://www.forbes.com/sites/walterpavlo/2011/08/12/
pennsylvania-judge-gets-life-sentence-for-prison-kickback-
scheme/

What is especially bothersome about this example is that Ciavarella carried out multiple and intentional miscarriages of justice to adult and juvenile defendants with no serious opposition to his corruption. His is not a unique case of judicial misconduct. There were no legal "brakes" to prevent his numerous misdeeds. The work group did nothing to stop him from corrupting the judicial process and if one thing is assured, *"they knew about it at some level."*

A part of this aura of invulnerability is derived from the election process for judges and prosecutors. In most states a voter is not allowed to know much of anything about candidates running for either office. The incumbent usually has the edge, however, because he can put the magical word – "re-elect" – in his campaign slogan. Otherwise, we know virtually nothing about the values, skills, and ideologies of these candidates. Instead of meaningful information the voters get visual promos that invariably include a smiling candidate with the following cues:

1. Candidate in a dark blue suit or powder blue shirt and khaki pants (standard issue uniform for business and politicos), and sometimes rolled-up sleeves (casual look).
2. An American flag in the background.
3. A dog (a showcase dog not a slobbering, flea infested pitbull.)
4. Smiling wife and children also dressed for the photo, clean cut and fresh underwear (we assume) and maybe
5. Religious reference tucked away in the photo e.g. "Blessed are the (heterosexual) beekeepers in the Garden of Eden."
6. Then, a slogan to tie the images together:
   "I promise to keep our city safe from criminals!"
   "Just call me Maximum Leo. Maximum penalties for every criminal."
   "I love the law, this country, and my wife's breast implants. God bless America and me."

"This job is a stepping stone for me to climb the political ladder."

"You do not know fuck all about me. Let's keep it that way. I am a good guy. Trust me."

This lack of useful knowledge at election time about judicial candidates wanting, aching to join the local courtroom work group is an open-door invitation for wholesale abuse and corruption. Campaign donors contribute because they damn well expect some benefits in civil (and criminal) court for themselves whether it involves favorable rulings on dangerous company practices or having a judge or prosecutor of the "same mindset" preside over their case in the future:

http://www.theatlantic.com/politics/archive/2014/10/courting-corruption-the-auctioning-of-the-judicial-system/381524/

To reiterate, the courtroom work group is an ensemble of actors of which the judge and prosecutor are the most potent. We elect them but know next to zero about their views of fairness, justice, and ethical standards. We hope they will be fair but, frankly, there is very little the common citizen can do about it if these judicial actors overstep their authority or turn into crooks (ditto for politicians as we wait for the "next best thing" in candidates). A few judges and prosecutors are disbarred and removed from office annually. A very few go to prison and even fewer are sanctioned or disciplined by state boards, councils, or commissions. At the federal level in 2012, for instance, 1,364 complaints were filed against federal judges. 1,352 were terminated (read=dead ended). That left 4 cases in which a Special Investigating Committee was appointed. Four cases out of 1,364 complaints.

http://www.uscourts.gov/statistics-reports/complaints-against-judges-judicial-business-2012

If there are solutions to the serious problems of work groups without oversight, of poor defendants badgered into plea deals (and the stigma of conviction), malfeasance by the actors, and similar issues, it will not probably occur within the criminal justice system. Billboard commissions and new task forces will be announced and officials will be climbing over one another before the cameras to frown and state (unequivocally) that "We must be diligent in upholding the rights of all citizens, blah, blah…" You can fill in the blanks on the soundbites later. Some new laws may be enacted but given the fact that legislators are typically composed of lawyers and business persons, exactly how much reform are you expecting? Lawyers and judges and business persons do not regulate their professions diligently, nor report their rare reviews of misconduct out to the public. Unless you believe that these judicial actors really are icons of virtue, in which case consider these two ready examples to the contrary:

> *"Charles Sebesta is a former Texas prosecutor who was disbarred for withholding evidence and using false testimony to secure the murder conviction of Anthony Graves, who was later exonerated after spending years in prison."*

*http://www.businessinsider.com/a-texas-prosecutor-who-with-held-evidence-to-win-a-murder-conviction-just-lost-his-law-license-2015-6#ixzz3ggPsvYMJ*

> *"After literally years of alleged misconduct involving jail-house informants, as well as prosecutors' repeated fail-ures to turn over exculpatory material, Judge Goethals determined in March that the office can simply no longer work on the case of mass murderer Scott Dekraai, who pleaded guilty last year to killing his ex-wife and seven others at a beauty salon."*

*http://www.slate.com/articles/news_and_politics/jurispru-dence/2015/05/orange_county_prosecutor_misconduct_judge_goethals_takes_district_attorney.single.html*

As distressing as rigged elections, a work group acting in their own interests, and hard boiled treatment of indigents can be, it all pales in comparison to the overarching issue of false positives and gross corruption within the judicial process that leads to disastrous outcomes.

# Wrongful Convictions / Wrongful Executions

> *"Wrongful convictions happen every week in every state in this country. And they happen for all the same reasons. Sloppy police work. Eyewitness identification is the most -*

*is the worst type almost. Because it's wrong about half the time. Think about that."*

*John Grisham*

It is difficult to fathom the feeling of being falsely accused and convicted. According to the National Registry of Exonerations, 1,628 people have been exonerated or "cleared" of their convictions.

*http://www.law.umich.edu/special/exoneration/Documents/ Exonerations_in_2013_Report.pdf*

The causes of wrongful convictions are legion; perjury, mistaken eyewitness identification, misconduct by police and prosecutors, tainted evidence, among others. 330 people have been exonerated (after conviction) through DNA evidence with an average of 14 years served before clearance and release from prison.

*Two Brooklyn Men Finally Exonerated of 1992 Murder*

> *"Everton Wagstaffe and Reginald Connor, two Brooklyn men found guilty of kidnapping in 1993, were finally fully exonerated on July 27th after an intermediate New York appeals court denied the state's motion to reargue an earlier decision reversing their convictions and dismissing the indictments against them based on prosecu-torial misconduct. Connor*

*served 15 years in prison and Wagstaffe served 23 years."*

*http://www.innocenceproject.org/*

1,628 is not a statistically significant number (statisticians are fond of the word – significant). I suspect no statistician has ever been wrongfully convicted; he/she might feel differently about the significance of that number. That number tells us that various courtroom work groups and actors, including the police, have made intentional, sometimes accidental mistakes with the evidence and, by extension, the accused in many jurisdictions. Moreover, these 1,628 mistakes are only those of which we are aware. It is "statistically probable" and highly likely, that more convicted defendants are yet to be identified as innocent.

*"For more than 35 years, a Texas man has been in a prison even though an appeals court threw out his conviction on a 1976 murder charge that initially had him on death row."*

http://news.yahoo.com/35-years-served-without-conviction-man-gets-trial-162142977.html

These unsettling conclusions about miscarriages of justice beg a number of questions. How many more innocent but convicted people are awaiting freedom? How is it that no criminal justice agency at any level of jurisdiction or author-ity had ever bothered to systematically investigate these cases? The Innocence Project and similar groups (few in number) serve as counterweights to an indifferent or incapable judi-cial system, one that grinds out plea bargains for major and minor offenses with insufficient attention to the possibility that someone may be innocent. Granted, many defendants did exactly what they were charged with, and probably more, but the filters for processing cases for the post-conviction reviews are badly in need of repair, especially in regards to the validity of DNA testing. One last question, the most dreadful of them all, needs to be asked.

How many wrongfully convicted people have been exe-cuted in America? 155 people on death row have been exon-erated since 1973:

http://www.deathpenaltyinfo.org/innocence-and-death-penalty

We do assume that some innocent people have been executed since 1900 and that other instances of justice gone wildly awry with death row convictions will be unearthed over time. Under the protection of qualified immunity, none of the judicial actors have much to worry about should they twist the truth (evidence) to gain a death penalty conviction. The defendant will have to rely on the appellate process for relief or the hopeful intervention of outside help such as The Innocence Project. The former is of no value to the defendant as they sit in their cells. Consider the case of Mr. Lorenzo Johnson:

*http://www.huffingtonpost.com/lorenzo-johnson/when-prosecu-tors-deny-jus_b_7713740.html*

Returning briefly to the problems of false positives and incorrect DNA matches, we know that state and the FBI crime labs have been consistently making errors in their assessment of evidence. This includes numerous technical mistakes and false or misleading reports provided to law enforcement and prosecutors by hundreds of public and private labs throughout the country. The outcomes of such misconduct are staggering e.g. loss of faith in the police and courts, but chief of those is conviction of the innocent:

> *"A former chemist for the state of Massachusetts' crime labs pleaded guilty Friday to falsifying drugs tests that potentially compromised tens of thousands of criminal cases. WBUR reports she admitted all 27 counts against her."*

http://www.npr.org/sections/thetwo-way/2013/11/22/246739071/chemist-pleads-guilty-in-massachusetts-crime-lab-scandal

This is not a solitary case. The FBI, for example, has admitted that its federal crime lab has been guilty of forensic mistakes for at least two decades. These mistakes such as flawed forensic testimony and convictions based on incorrect lab results date back, it appears, to at least the 1980's.

> *"The inquiry includes 2,600 convictions and 45 death-row cases from the 1980s and 1990s in which the FBI's hair and fiber unit reported a match to a crime-scene sample before DNA testing of hair became common. The FBI had reviewed about 160 cases before it stopped, officials said."*

http://www.washingtonpost.com/local/crime/federal-review-stalled-after-finding-forensic-errors-by-fbi-lab-unit-spanned-two-decades/2014/07/29/04ede880-11ee-11e4-9285-4243a40ddc97_story.html?wpsrc=AG0003376

Private and public crime labs have been at fault in most states; this lack of oversight is not surprising since not all labs are accredited and monitored for using proper evaluative protocols. Labs typically work for and report to law enforcement. Some labs get paid by the conviction rate. It is known as funding through court-assessed fees; for every person implicated in a crime the lab receives a fee, sometimes paid for by the accused. This includes charges ranging from DUI to capital murder. Thus, for those labs, a very clear bias exists. Their budgets (and salaries) are linked to the volume of charges that produce fees. Those results also convict the innocent as we saw in a more notorious case involving the State Bureau of Crime Lab in North Carolina:

*"The report found that SBI agents withheld exculpatory evidence or distorted evidence in more than 230 cases over a 16-year period. Three of those cases resulted in execution. There was widespread lying, corruption, and pressure from prosecutors and other law enforcement officials on crime lab analysts to produce results that would help secure convictions. And the pressure worked."*

http://reason.com/archives/2010/08/23/north-carolinas-corrupted-crim

Corrupt crime labs? Tainted evidence? Payment for false positive results? Unqualified technicians and no oversight. Whew! That's a lot of awful to digest. So, like many other myths discussed, it is time to abandon this one by the railroad tracks. Crime labs are often wrong in their findings and the result is corrosive to every basic principle of justice. Sometimes the wrong people get convicted and, worse, sometimes the judicial process and its actors are entirely to blame for the disastrous outcomes.

# Maxim

I had hoped to say something witty about how justice is administered in America but the words escape me. The images of a courtroom work group acting in collusion and in their own best interests ("your honor, when is your tee time today?"), poor defendants rotting in jails because they are indigent and unable to pay a meager cash bond, the widespread practice of cheating and "fudging" crime lab results in order to get paid and get convictions, and the notion that innocent people periodically are charged, convicted and incarcerated, makes me giddy with confusion. Is this how justice is doled out in an oligarchic society? How many lies can we tell before the myths disappear and the truths are revealed about a skewed playing field in the courts of justice? Sweet Kahuna, how and when does this whirlwind of police falsehoods and calculated judicial corruption end?

How often do we need to be shown that the justice system is in gross disrepair before changes are made to fix the problems? These problems and errors are fixable, have no doubts on that point, but few if any positive reforms will ever be implemented by those in charge of the madhouse. How can it possibly be in their best interests to repair the broken bits of the judicial process if the current modus operandi (method of operation) works so exclusively and well to their benefit?

Perhaps one small side, closing anecdote might be in order about the human nature of courtroom actors. A judge / colleague went through a very bitter divorce and he lost everything but his shoes in the final disposition. His anger was mirrored in his face and his voice echoed with confusion and deep resentment. He mentioned in a later conversation, with a wide grin, that he was being reassigned for the upcoming calendar year. To divorce court…That probably turned out poorly for someone. I hate to think how he would have acted presiding over a criminal court.

Looking Elsewhere
http://www.nacdl.org/criminaldefense.aspx?id=28286

http://www.businessinsider.com/forensic-csi-crime-labs-disaster-2014-4

<u>Thin Blue Line (film):</u> Be sure to watch the closing fifteen minutes.

# Seven

## U.S. SUPREME COURT: THE GREATEST GIG IN THE GALAXY

*"Free speech has been used by the Supreme Court to give immense power to the wealthiest members of our society."*

NOAM CHOMSKY

## Help Wanted!!!

Forget cobbling together two, three part-time jobs without benefits or safe working conditions. Forget sustainable wages, that chimera of false hopes so proudly touted by economists and people with guaranteed jobs. Search no further, my friend, for that dream job! We are looking, every 20-30 years, for that "special person" to join our very small, secluded, elite group of nine judges. You must be from an ivy-league school, lived with either a silver spoon in your mouth or golden nets to catch you in the event of failure. And preferably well connected via family and law school hook-ups. In short, not one of the "common sort" who ride public transport to work or whose children attend public schools.

Specific qualifications include:

- White middle-aged males with receding hairlines preferred but am willing to consider older female applicants of multiple status categories e.g. lesbian, Samoan, Muslim, left handed, and only slightly outspoken.
- You must be from an ivy-league school law school, lived with either a silver spoon provided at birth, a solid portfolio of investments, and a respectable trust fund to tide one over in the event of another stock market crash.
- Well connected via family and law school hook-ups (high-profile patrons are required).
- Able to interpret the United States Constitution in such a way that it promotes your own personal values and political viewpoints within the context of legal language and logic.
- Poor, state law school graduates without the advantage of being from elite schools and privileged lifestyles need not apply. Besides, you would not look right in the team photos.
- Able to appear unbiased and fair when reviewing the facts of legally disputed conflicts.

- Required that all applicants must be of the identical party and political affiliation as the reigning President. Easy access to and face time with members of the United States Congress is an additional bonus.
- Editor of a law school review is helpful as is publication of an article on an esoteric topic such as "Hidden loopholes of the tax code paradigm introduced and exploited by three of my ancestors during President Grant Administration, with particular focus on ways to capitalize one's savings account by using glass beads to purchase wholesale acreage from Native Americans."

Benefits:

- $200,000 guaranteed annual salary that can never be reduced, only increased.
- Lifetime full medical benefits including dental and vision care.
- Federal pension upon retirement.
- Nine-month work year. Extremely flexible hours. Work from home as often as you wish.
- Opportunities for multiple, generous "honorariums" for speaking engagements (scripts provided), lectures at foreign law schools / conferences (per diem costs, first-class travel, and speaking fees), and many more.
- Positions on national boards upon retirement with hefty salaries and compensation.

- Complete independence from any type of oversight and accountability. Nobody, and we include the baby Jesus, Mohammad, Congress, and the United Nations can reprimand you. Ever.
- Work as many or as few hours as you wish. Hey, toss back another espresso and roll in about 10:00 a.m., water the plants, lift some files (whew, these legal briefs are heavy!), and call it a day by 1:00 p.m.
- People shut up when you speak. We do ask that you refrain from bitch slapping visitors or the press if they prove irritating. Good manners, after all, are a sign of good breeding. Besides, you can mock the citizenry after they leave the room.
- A full staff to attend to all of your needs. Massages are optional. Trampoline workouts and use of the court hot tub, are permitted provided you sign a liability waiver.
- Year-round, free, reserved parking.
- Access to a private gymnasium for one's daily high impact work-out routine.
- You can NEVER be fired or removed from this job, short of impeachment and that is as likely to happen as a pregnant nun appearing with an immaculate conception, which is say – not ever. Fall asleep during oral arguments on major issues on such topics as abortion, NSA surveillance programs, gun control? No worries! Your colleagues will cover for you. Get seriously ill during a session of the court? No worries! You can never be replaced until you resign or die.

> There are still some pending legal arguments about whether dead justices can serve if their phantoms appear for work.

Apply immediately to the President of the United States upon public notice of a vacancy in the United States Supreme Court.

There are probably not that many top tier jobs that are as deliciously cushy and rock hard sexy as being a member of the U.S. Supreme Court. That court has only nine members. Think about that. This job has had only 112 or so employees in 225 years. Being a judge on that bench is the pinnacle of judicial power; money, prestige (clients come to you cap in hand!!!), perks galore, front row seats to heavyweight boxing, and a workload that would make a New Jersey union dockworker envious. The Supreme Court picks and chooses which cases to review and a one-hundred decision caseload or so each year (term) is considered - "bonus satis" or good enough. That does not mean the court actually hands down a decision in each case. It means it "considers" doing something which is equivalent to almost getting out of bed each morning to go to work. Naturally, when criticized for being such lightweights with their caseload, the justice invariably respond – "You just don't understand the job! It is much harder than you think." Frankly, justices, and with all due respect for the court, I do think my bullshit alarm is shrieking about now.

If that sounds a bit harsh please note that each justice of the Supreme Court has clerks from the top law schools in the nation who do most of the administrative legwork. They prepare cases for review, take out the trash, change the bog paper in the marbled restrooms, and keep the docket (list of pending cases) in running order. Moreover, these aspiring wannabe power players – clerks write summaries of cases and even help draft written opinions on some cases. They serve as key discretionary filters that have the ears of judges and whisper sweet nothings about issues from time to time ("don't forget me boss when I need a job reference."). Unlike us who only whisper sweet somethings to ourselves aka "I rule in favor of myself!", the judges have buckets of time to tackle a larger workload but the law does not require it and sometimes it makes excellent sense for the court to STFU on issues that are bitterly contested e.g. gun control, abortion, Common Cause standards. It is similar to being a parent who is expected to preside over one's children knowing full well that no matter what you say or do one of the little buggers is going to get riled and bite the neighbor's kid. In short, the court knows that two parties enter the cage of constitutional challenges but only one emerges victorious. Regrettably the plaintiffs do not get to use fisticuffs and nut kicking to sort out their differences.

What, therefore, do we know about the internal machinery of this extremely powerful, influential august body of judges?

Not much. About as much as we know about the location of Atlantis and the reasons why Minnesota was ever declared a state. They remain mysteries in both instances.

# The Cheesecake Theory of Crime

The process by which nine Supreme Court judges evaluate and make (or not) decisions about profound topics such as slavery, the death penalty, abortion, conscription, and many others, is basically a grand illusion to us. That process of review is a closed door proceeding. Ideally, the justices exist in some ethereal plane of total objectivity. Wisdom, fairness, and justice are dispensed with benevolent, loving smiles. Wrongs are righted and seldom is heard a discouraging word and the skies are not cloudy all day. That is known as the myth of judicial benevolence. Would that it was so and the court could pack its collective lunch pails and go home every term with a feeling of a job well done. Cue James Brown – "I Feel Good!!!!!!!!!!!!!" Go home to martinis on the veranda at the summer homes and a visit from their financial advisors via helicopters ("Have you seen the traffic in the city?! Goodness!").

The reality is a tad different, however, and the tad is much like learning the neighbors shot, skinned, and ate the Easter Bunny for dinner.

The method by which judges determine which cases to hear and decide upon is equivalent to placing a bet on a roulette wheel. These are very long odds (absurd actually) of guessing correctly. There are tales of midnight sessions with the nine judges huddled around an Ouija board, incense burning in the background, and lots of Tibetan chanting. At least I can relate to that approach. However, predictions of what cases will actually make it to oral arguments and for what reasons are the breadsticks and butter living of media mouthpieces, consultants (read=unable to find gainful employment), and professors of Political Science. The court owes us no explanations. It can ignore any requests for answers as to what it does. Justices hold their posts until death (or the embalming fluid kicks in) and according to the Constitutional standard of "good behavior". None of the justices have ever been forcibly removed or impeached no matter how outrageous or outlandish their decisions and behavior. If the reader detects a note of envy, so be it. Even U.S. Congressmen who are caught with drunken strippers in public fountains or both hands in the public till of bribery cannot compete with the U.S. Supreme Court for sheer arrogance of power and influence. Equally noteworthy, no justice is beholden to any other branch of government and need not solicit campaign contributions or support from anyone or any group.

This judicial gang is the third branch of the government tripod. The judges are independent, autonomous, untouchable, and completely unrepresentative of the society they are supposed to serve. The court is the embodiment of entitlement whose members (with a few noteworthy exceptions) spring from the loins of the landed gentry of this nation. There is no method or mechanism for removing a judge who suffers a permanent or disabling illness. Short of impeachment, which has never occurred, a justice cannot be compelled to resign. A few have been known to fall asleep during oral arguments and frankly, who can blame them given their backbreaking workload and the mind-numbingly dull ramblings of attorneys arguing before the court? To wit:

# The Cheesecake Theory of Crime

"Your honors, we stand before you hoping you will concur in striking down the civil rights of all people who are not white, male, heterosexual, Christian, and Good Americans. Failing that, my client and his followers would like your permission to worship poisonous snakes, play with fire and drink strychnine while speaking in tongues during church services." Pause. "What's that, your honor? That is already allowed in North Carolina? Hmm, I did not know that."

Visit the four-story building which houses the U.S. Supreme Court. It has a classical design and interior aesthetic that drips of Roman orgies and bad taste. There will be no loud farts in this building, thankee very much. Marble statutes, ceilings so high they have cloud formations, and sprays of Latin sprinkled about create an atmosphere of formal dignity and reserve much like the funeral of a stranger or a family reunion when everybody is trying hard not to acknowledge how fat the others have become. Inside that fortress of justice one might stumble upon the private gymnasium, restaurant (?), massive law library, separate offices, multiple meeting rooms, staff support offices, casino, coffee bar, and discounted guns and ammo shop (I am guessing with the last three items). Plus the court does have its own police force and free, ample parking for all justices. The latter is an almost priceless perk in Washington, D.C., as you might guess. Besides, do we really want these nine robed judges riding a city bus to work or jockeying for a metered parking spot somewhere in the wilds of Washington?

Who are these people? Until fairly recently almost all Supreme Court judges have been white, middle-aged males of privileged backgrounds. Today's bench consists of nine judges who are all millionaires, thus making them exactly unlike the majority of people (the electorate) that they represent. Except for the 10% or so of the nation's families who own most of the collective wealth and assets and direct the political processes (did you really belief your vote made a difference in any election outside of local government?), the U.S. Supreme Court speaks for… well, let's just say most of us will never be on their Xmas card list. There is no way to know exactly how much each is worth as they are not required, unlike other earth-bound citizens, to provide disclosures of their entire financial portfolio. Also, a portion of their wealth can be transferred to a spouse or a trust fund and thus is not reportable. The best guesses are that the poorest judge is worth two million plus chump change and the richest are sitting on seven, eight million dollars. These are considered to be a very conservative estimates. Several judges apparently do have extensive holdings in stocks and bonds. That means if a case / plaintiff appears before them in which one or more judges owns stock he / she must recuse (hide in a closet) him/herself.

> "The enemy is within the gates; it is with our own luxury, our own folly, our own criminality that we have to contend."
>
> Marcus Tullius Cicero

The current bench of judges consists of Ivy League law school graduates; Harvard (5), Yale (3), and Columbia (1). It is no longer exclusively male dominated; three women are justices. It is also no longer an all-white club. One judge is black and he is dynamic, engaging, and a pro-minority rights advocate. Actually, he is a laconic, marginal judge who is glaringly absent on issues involving minority rights. His few judicial evaluations read like a blind man advocating for the rights of "seeing" people. The average age is 69. And they are all inhaling oxygen, dining at the right restaurants, and in possession of a major league rolodex of contacts. But that's about it as far as representation goes. These folks entered the legal fast track of career advancement just in the historical time and circumstances necessary to be nominated by the President.

In return, these judges implicitly agree to side with the prevailing ideology that got them the court job. With some wriggle room for the odd dissent or two. That makes sense. Why nominate your enemies to a job where they can never be fired or give them the means to do your cause irreparable harm? After all, there is no way to sack this band of jugglers for poor performances.

What kind of bang for the buck do we get from this quasi- neutral, sort of fair, aristocratic bench of intelligent, nine learned souls? The United States Supreme Court can only address cases that work their way up through the appeals process beginning with the verdict in trial court. There have been some marvelous but deeply overdue decisions that are part of our civil rights. Periodically the U.S. Supreme Court has handed down some etched in stone landmark decisions that have transformed, for better or worse, the legal panorama of our country. Decisions involving the rights of the accused (Miranda v. Arizona, et al), abortion (Roe v. Wade), the Exclusionary Rule (Mapp v. Ohio, et al.) are a few examples of the court's ability to intervene into the lives and rights of citizens, often to very good effect. Contrary to those neo-Nazi officials who advocate waterboarding and station house beatings to extract confessions, the rights of the accused matter a great deal if the heartbeat of public order is to be maintained without adrenaline injections. But, this is not to say that the court has been squatting in the dugouts with us, sweating out the small things like institutional racism, gun control, strict liability for corporations, civil forfeiture, the right to die, and many other concerns too numerous to mention. No, not when you have reserved parking in Washington, D.C. You do not sweat the small stuff. The result of being so very omnipotent, or thinking one is, is the uncanny aptitude for making judicial errors. I refer to some exceptional, boneheaded decisions.

<u>Buck v. Bell</u>, 1927
*"Three generations of imbeciles are enough".*
Justice Holmes

*"We have seen more than once that the public welfare may call upon the best citizens for their lives. It would be strange if it could not call upon those who already sap the strength of the State for these lesser sacrifices, often not felt to be such by those concerned, to prevent our being swamped with*

*incompetence. It is better for all the world, if instead of waiting to execute degenerate offspring for crime, or to let them starve for their imbecility, society can prevent those who are manifestly unfit from continuing their kind. The principle that sustains compulsory vaccination is broad enough to cover cutting the Fallopian tubes."*

(Chief Justice Wendell Holmes aka Judge "Tainted Love")

Read this one again and cogitate. Carrie Buck was an 18-year-old female declared mentally inferior and promiscuous and involuntarily sterilized in Virginia. This decision was used to launch and support a smorgasbord of programs that resulted in approximately 60,000 – 70,000 involuntary sterilizations of male and females throughout 30 states. That is considered a low estimate. The eugenics movement was wildly popular and a draconian version was introduced by some Harvard graduates (thanks fellas!) who felt that the rich were intellectually superior people. It behooves us, so the thinking went, to cleanse society of retarded, disabled, low IQ, poor, racially inferior families by "regulating" their reproductive rights. In North Carolina, a classy state by anyone's standards that still thinks it is 1864 and the Union Army is threatening Raleigh, anyone with a certified IQ below 70 (which should have qualified all of the vanilla wafer legislators and bankers and tobacco tycoons) was eligible for sterilization. The U.S. Supreme Court has yet to overturn the full terms of the decision in Buck v. Bell. You read that right. In some milder forms, the states retain the authority to sterilize its citizens. I am not sure how pro-gun advocates will feel about that one? Castrate us – okay. Take our guns? – no sirree, Bob!!!

As a wistful side note, our eugenics movement and philosophy became an inspirational theme for the Nazis who credited the United States with the reasoning for developing a superior race through "science." We saw how that panned out to the horror and extinction of millions of Jews.

Nice work, judges. You too Judge Holmes. It is a pity you did not qualify as a "defective" so you could share the experience of involuntary sterilization along with Ms. Buck. Sans the anesthesia.

## Dred Scott v. Sandford 1857

This is a classic case chewed up in law schools. Chief Justice Roger Taney declared in a 7-2 decision that all people of African descent, free or slaves, living within the United States were slaves forever and not entitled to basic rights or protections. Black people, regardless of free status reverted to slave status (property) and could be treated as chattel. I give you one guess how this panned out.

Four years later, in 1861, the Civil War began. One of the overarching issues of that ghastly conflict was emancipation and a determination of the basic rights of all people. Fuck the issue of state's rights. Does anyone with both sides of their brain intact truly believe that eventually all of the slave holding states would voluntarily surrender the plantation system and emancipate their slaves because it was the right and just thing to do? Believe it or not, that remains an ongoing debate. If slavery is such a proper and beneficial condition why should whites not participate as slaves in order to receive some of the God-ordained rights and "perks" of being a non-citizen? Hmm...I do not see a line of white people forming to test out this idea. Apparently Justice Taney (and Justice Holmes) would find advocates of slavery today in Florida, Texas, North Carolina, Mississippi, Virginia, Tennessee, and South Carolina. Sweat shops that produce cheap clothes for major retail stores in America, migrant field workers who get coated with pesticides by crop dusters, child labor in fourth world nations e.g. Haiti, sexual trafficking of children and women – sounds like slavery to me.

The Dred Scott decision has a brutal finality to it that required a nation wrenched in two by a massive bloodletting known as the Civil War (1861-1864). The South aka Confederate States of America lost but the racial hatred simmers and periodically rears its deformed face to the world. Justice Taney was a racist, mean, ignorant white asshole who helped light the fuse to a powder keg of death and destruction. He tried to formalize the idea that black people could never receive due process or relief within the criminal justice systems. He also had wagon loads of supporters which we call "Tea Baggers" and right-wing Republicans. Those who are still apologizing for slavery and want to dole out money to black people as compensation are called Democrats. These groups are rarely seen in the same public swimming pool.

Glossip v. Gross, 2015

With this last case, chosen for its novelty, the Supreme Court ruled that Midazolam, a sedative used to calm an inmate during lethal injection along with two other drugs (part of a three-drug protocol) did not constitute cruel and unusual punishment, even if the drugs did not work as anticipated. This case was originally titled Warner v. Gross but Charles Warner was executed while waiting for the Supreme Court to review his appeal. Ouch! It would have been fun to see their expressions had they ruled in Warner's favor without realizing he had been executed. "He's dead? My, this is awkward. Is a fibulator out of the question?" It does seem to be true that sometimes the wheels of justice turn ever so slowly...

*"(b) Petitioners failed to establish that any risk of harm was substantial when compared to a known and available alternative method of execution "*

## GLOSSIP ET AL. *v.* GROSS ET AL.
## CERTIORARI TO THE UNITED STATES
## COURT OF APPEALS FOR THE TENTH CIRCUIT
No. 14–7955.  Argued April 29, 2015—
Decided June 29, 2015

The case was renamed Glossip v. Gross but, as one can see, the same outcome awaits Mr. Gross. He is scheduled to be executed on September 16th, 2015 in the State of Oklahoma. There remain some valid, unanswered questions about Mr. Glossip's guilt. The Supreme Court, keep in mind, need not review any death penalty appeals. Is this a great job or what?

# Maxim

The Supreme Court of the United States (SCOTUS) is not omnipotent or remotely representative of its constituents, the electorate. It is an elite branch of the federal government composed primarily of nine people from privileged backgrounds with the proper political alignment and timing to be nominated. Presidents have tried to stack this court with friendly minds. This court lives in the rarified air of invulnerability. Not one justice has ever been removed from office. These are nine untouchable federal employees who preside over the most complex, urgent questions confronting society such as:

- Redistricting (designed to keep incumbents in office).
- Voter registration laws (designed to place obstacles to voting).
- Presidential vote counts in Florida (Mr. Bush sends his thanks).
- The legality of torture (waterboarding, electrocution).
- Right to privacy v. constant digital surveillance by the National Security Agency and other government units.
- Legality of invading other countries without a formal declaration of war.
- Police powers.

- Campaign contributions (at present – unlimited amounts may be donated to candidates from a secret sources. That should work out well, eh?).
- Deciding who owns outer space and can parts of it be sold by mega-corporations to third world nations?
- Right to die for terminally ill citizens. Why is this still an issue?
- Restitution for wrongful convictions.

This is a very short list of issues but, nor worries, because the court is not going to rule on them anytime soon. Maybe it is just as well that the SCOTUS is a bunch of untouchable emus that few would recognize in the grocery store. They frequently speak in defense of the "non-liability" of corporations and other fixed-in-cement icons of society such as tax-exempt religions, charities, legislatures, and federal agencies. They do so with vigor and conviction. Sometimes, however, (actually often), I yearn for a Supreme Court made up of educators, coaches, morticians, plumbers, night-school lawyers instead of the rigorously guarded applicants and pathways to the court. That is my prejudice, however, and I stick to it.

What we deserve, instead of landed gentry on the bench are intelligent, capable individuals who have no ties to donors, political parties or the 10%. You know, people with a grounding in reality. These are people who understand that being beholden to and part of the privileged layer of society is nothing to boast about or exploit. Keep the process of appointment intact but broaden the playing field of candidates to include the "common man and woman." That might produce some very refreshing nominations instead of the predictable conveyor belt of cookie cutter applicants from privileged settings...

## Looking Elsewhere

http://www.supremecourt.gov/

http://www.uscourts.gov/

http://caselaw.findlaw.com/court/us-supreme-court

# Eight

HOME AWAY FROM HOME: PRISONS,
JAILS, AND FEMALE OFFENDERS

*"There must be some kind of way out
of here, said the joker to the thief."*

PURPLE HAZE, JIMMY HENDRIX

No one volunteers to be locked away but some of us must be incarcerated for two valuable reasons:

1) Society needs a goddamn break, some relief, from the bullies, thieves, gangsters, rapists, killers, child molesters, identity thieves and sundry other fun fest folks who really know how to put the "id" in idiot." We need these people to go away now, preferably out of sight and sound (which is why prisons are often placed in rural settings) and stop hurting us. At least we know where to find you in case a zombie apocalypse erupts.

# The Cheesecake Theory of Crime

During the course of my field work as a researcher and investigator I visited a wide variety of correctional institutions. Without exception I became depressed and blank faced shortly after entry among the general population. The noise levels were invasive, profanities bellowed like lines from a rehearsal of Shakespeare's lesser-known literary efforts titled: "Fuck you motherfucker Hamlet fucking yeah in the ass punk motherfucker!" It was not one of his better plays. A prison/jail aesthetic is a palette of dark colors nestled within the echoes of heavy doors locking in place, the shouts of inmates and staff, and the heady aromas of intense body stink. You would never want to wave an ultra-violet (UV) light anywhere in these facilities. Some stains are best left undiscovered. There are some exceptions but within these closed communities, much like an urban zoo, the animals keep a very close eye on their keepers. Inmates, by the way, monitor everything that happens within their environment. They watch and wait for opportunities.

2) Revenge. Pain is not the exclusive domain of criminals. Society demands its bucket of blood and guts from people who mistreat us. We want the offenders to feel as badly as the victims. That is why we have the criminal justice system to act on our behalf and no, we have zero expectations of your success with rehabilitation.

The branch of criminal justice responsible for the administration of convicted citizens is called Corrections. About 6.9

million persons were under the supervision of adult correctional systems in 2013. This supervision occurs in several ways; institutions (prisons, jails, work farms), community placement (probation), and mixed (a bit of both e.g. parole, halfway houses). Some sentences are issued for community service and the offender must spend X number of hours working in non-profit settings for free (pro bono). This is a simplified version of corrections and includes some equally blunt figures for 2013.

- 1 in 110 adults were incarcerated in prison or local jail.
- 1 in 51 adults were on probation or parole.
- State and federal correctional facilities held about 1,574,700 prisoners, an increase of 4,300 prisoners.
- The United States of America, that bastion of individual liberties and human rights locks up and supervises more convicted citizens than any other nation in the world. GO TEAM USA!!! Thomas Jefferson and the Fathers of the Constitution would be mightily impressed assuming, of course, that they could take some time off from running their slave plantations to applaud our success in sticking people in steel cells.
- Black males (about 12% of the population) represent almost half of the total correctional population.
- In 2011–12, about 40% of state and federal prisoners and jail inmates reported having a current chronic medical condition.

http://www.bjs.gov/index.cfm?ty=tp&tid=1

# The Cheesecake Theory of Crime

Corrections is the tail end of the judicial dog. The four goals of punishment in our criminal justice system still in use are:

1. Deterrence; The assumption is that people are deterred from committing crimes because of the promise of punishment. Maybe for some but not for all. Besides, prisons and jail provide loads of opportunities for crimes (in addition to yoga and crafts classes of course). The beat of crime is not interrupted by deterrence. We only wish it were so. Remember one of my cardinal principles of crime and punishment – we pick and choose which crimes we intend to break.

2. Punishment; Nothing subtle here. Wham! Bam! Pain in equal measure for the pain someone has inflicted someone else or group e.g. church shootings.. This can take a number of forms including fines, probation, electronic monitoring, and a favorite – solitary confinement. The research on solitary confinement is very conclusive. Installing someone in a segregated cell with no stimuli or company is a fast track to insanity and suicides and all manner of awful mental disorders.

*"When corrections officials talk about solitary confinement, they describe it as the prison within the prison, and for good reason. For 23 hours a day, inmates are kept inside a cell that is approximately 80 square feet, smaller than a typical horse stable. Cells are furnished*

*with a bed, sink and toilet, but rarely much else. Food is delivered through a slot in the door, and each day inmates are allowed just one hour of exercise, in a cage."*

http://www.pbs.org/wgbh/pages/frontline/criminal-justice/locked-up-in-america/what-does-solitary-confinement-do-to-your-mind/

3. Incapacitation; Locked up somewhere with ample time to meditate upon what went wrong and "how can I become a productive member of society". This remains the most costly option of the four goals and, arguably, the least effective. Its two main perks are: (1) the true offender is not able to hurt us while incarcerated and; (2) We steal their lives by depriving them of years of their existence that could have been spent in free society. Prisons and jail are time machines. Those inside know that life continues outside without them and they find ways to adapt to institutional care and security expectations. An inmate grows old within that facility; we hope he will emerge a changed man but the odds are too heavily stacked against success. The change, if it does happen, may be the result of –

4. Rehabilitation; Programs and services are offered e.g. job training, GED courses, meant to help an inmate or person on P&P (probation and parole) transition into a legitimate lifestyle. It is an uphill slog for many inmates because:

# The Cheesecake Theory of Crime

## 3 IN 4 FORMER PRISONERS IN 30 STATES ARRESTED WITHIN 5 YEARS OF RELEASE

*"WASHINGTON – An estimated two-thirds (68 percent) of 405,000 prisoners released in 30 states in 2005 were arrested for a new crime within three years of release from prison, and three-quarters (77 percent) were arrested within five years, the Bureau of Justice Statistics (BJS) announced today.*

*More than a third (37 percent) of prisoners who were arrested within five years of release were arrested within the first six months after release, with more than half (57 percent) arrested by the end of the first year."*

http://www.bjs.gov/content/pub/press/rprts05p0510pr.cfm

It is worth noting that a single conviction, including any type of property offense, greatly limits one's employment prospects, starting with the application paperwork.

*"Have you ever been convicted of a crime? If so, mark yes and explain in the box below. If yes, please describe the type and location of all tattoos and the contact information for 50 persons (with current phone numbers) who know you better than your family and are currently not in prison. Plus, accurately explain the nature of quantum physics within 25 words or less. In Arabic."*

Gainful employment for released ex-offenders is a zip line ride into a chasm. Not much hope for recovery and success which is no surprise since the barriers to re-entry are severe. They include, among others, the loss of visitation rights with their children, limits on signing contracts, no access to credit, poor work history, ban on voting, and a stigma that says – once an offender, always an offender. For some, being institutionalized gives a structure and order to their lives that was absent in the free world. For some, being locked up is a haven of sorts from an intolerable existence outside. And for a number of other inmates, being locked up is the only real life they have known as an adult; these people may someday "age out" of their sentence but there is no rainbow's pot of gold waiting upon their release. The recidivist rate or rate at which people re-commit crimes is the benchmark used to measure the success of our four goals and that rate is persistently high. We also measure success by our ability to contain convicts in a state or federal facility. We are very adept at keeping them in small, steel rooms. We take time and basic freedoms from them and most get released early from their sentences.

But the term corrections is a misnomer. Technically speaking, we do not correct anyone. We punish them and hope a few survivors e.g. property offenders, exit with a second chance at a normal life as taxpayers. This expectation, of course does not apply to white collar offenders since so very few of them are very arrested and "corrected" in the criminal justice system.

# Jails

The local version of corrections is the familiar jail. People sitting in a county or city jail are there for one year or less. Jails have historically served as a convenient dumpster for society's unwashed and unwanted citizens. Part asylum, part lockup, and one part certified landfill; jails in America have a well-earned reputation as a repository for people who fall in the category of "don't know what else to do with them." Unlike prisons, jails hold a percentage of people who:

- Await trial or arraignment and cannot afford bail or are considered too dangerous to be released on bail and pose a risk for flight. Arraignment means the defendant's right to know of the charges against him and his rights to have enough information to prepare a defense. It is specifically stated in the 6th Amendment to the Constitution; "…be informed of the nature and cause of the accusation against them." Preparing a defense from one's jail cell is hard to do (actually nigh impossible) without help from outsiders.
- Have violated the terms of their probation and parole agreements.
- Are mentally ill and need to be shipped to a mental health institution.
- Are juveniles awaiting placement.
- Await transfer to state or federal prisons.
- Got stuck in a jail because other facilities were too crowded ("sorry, but did you have a reservation?")

- Owe child support payments. As part of their sanction, the non-custodial parent is allowed to work during the week but must report to the jail on Friday evening and sit in a cell until release on Monday morning. His/her paycheck is garnished (diverted) to the custodial parent. Every weekend, throughout the country, the parking lots of jails host the migration of non-custodial parents entering and exiting the secure facility.
- Are actually innocent of the charges filed against them but cannot afford release on bail.
- Mentally retarded and special needs people who may or may not have done anything wrong. A common practice with some police departments and jails and was to drop these people off in other jurisdictions with a bus ticket and some cash.

Thus American jails are catch-all, big box type of institutions, with a soup to nuts clientele many of whom have no business being placed cheek to jowl with one another. In 2014 there were about 745,000 people locked in city and county jails. I would argue that many jails do a poor job of securing the rights and safety of their visitors, staff and residents simply because too much is expected of the facilities. Contagious diseases, psychotic episodes, high suicide rates, other violent outbursts, sexual assaults (by resident and staff), and public indifference to what happens within these places are a few of the problems confronting jails and their administration. A guiding principle of jails is called custodial convenience.

This means a jail provides a minimal level of service to the residents. The needs of the administration trump those of the incarcerated. Lots of very bad practices go uncorrected and I do not refer to spraying for cockroaches once a week or forgetting to put mint chocolates on the pillows of inmate beds at night. Actually, the truth is much more like this:

> *"Maryland's governor announced plans Thursday to immediately shut down Baltimore's state-run jail, where inmates and guards ran a criminal conspiracy inside vermin-infested, 19th-century walls and thwarted decades of attempted reforms."*

*https://news.yahoo.com/video/infamous-baltimore-prison-immediately-shut-175346866.html*

or this:

> *"NASHVILLE, Tenn. (AP) — Former inmates at a privately run Nashville jail say they worked without pay building bean-bag "cornhole" games, plaques shaped like footballs, birdhouses and dog beds so that officials could sell them through their personal business at a flea market."*

*http://news.yahoo.com/inmates-worked-free-jail-officials-180231802.html*

But especially like this…

# Whistleblowing in the Wind Tunnel of Justice

It was my bad fortune, fresh out of school, to work in a jail which practiced custodial convenience. And, for the first time, I am going to reveal my identity as the anonymous whistle-blower that helped launch a state investigation into the policies, incidents, and practices of that jail. Keep in mind that I was a freshly minted college graduate, optimistic, naïve, and stupid. My job included service as a deputy sheriff and correctional officer. My training was episodic and incomplete for both jobs. But hope springs eternal in the hearts of idiots like me. My former jail and bosses (sheriff and warden) permitted and perpetuated a slew of questionable and illegal practices. To wit:

- The warden's wife and his daughter prepared the daily meals. The warden was allotted a fixed amount of money for these meals, say $3 daily x the number of residents. Staff was also fed from the same "buffet" as the inmates. If the warden could provide these meals at a cost of $2 daily, the excess of one dollar could be "held back." So, let's do some simple math. On a typical weekend with a headcount of 50 we get: 50 inmates x $1 surplus x 30 days = $1,500. The meals routinely consisted of black coffee, white bread, jello, Twinkies, canned vegetables, sugared water, white rice, bologna, and crackers. I suspect the surplus money was placed back into the department budget.

- Suicides went unreported to the press. Suicides were made "easier" by the fact that we handed out double-edged razor blades every morning for shaving. To no one's surprise many of these deadly blades "went missing."

- Juveniles were placed in one of two small cells, sequestered by an iron door but not technically out of sight and sound, a requirements for placing juveniles in an adult facility. The cells included a seat-less toilet, metal bed, sink, and dim light in the narrow hall. During my one-year stint with this jail, I was present or knew of several suicides, self-mutilations, escape attempts, fires started by the occupants, and flooded cells.

- In this three-tiered jail I was also witness to attempted suicides, this time by adults, one of which resulted in injury to me (razor cuts by the inmate) as I blocked his attempt to completely slash open his wrists. In addition, sexual assaults and beatings happened periodically. The cellblocks were surrounded by thick, greasy, dark fencing, weak ventilation, and very dim overhead lights. One effect of that physical setup was that inmates could see the staff clearly as we made our rounds but we had only limited vision of what was happening inside the cellblocks.

- The cells could not be locked down for emergencies. All cells fed into a common room in the middle of each cell block. Vulnerable inmates could not be segregated.

- Female inmates occupied one large cell visible to all passersby. It was situated about 10 feet directly opposite the juvenile holding cells. A favorite trick of these inmates was to "drop the top" on their orange overalls, naked underneath, and offer sex to staff and other passing inmates.

- Mentally ill and retarded residents were placed in the drunk tank, usually without supervision or LOS (line of sight) and handcuffed until the shift supervisor could figure out what to do with them. This could take days.

- One reason for my dual role as cop and jailer was a chronic manpower shortage. We were expected to rotate back and forth between the two gigs. The jail was always shorthanded.

- Sometimes, if an arrestee was abusive or resisting booking he was beaten in an adjacent room. A drunken car dealer, for instance, was arrested for driving a Cadillac into a swimming pool in the dead of winter. He arrived in a short sleeved white shirt, glasses broken, and bruised from the crash. No medical care was offered. He refused to go quietly into the drunk tank and resisted the staff. He was unceremoniously hoisted off the ground by several officers, dragged into a nearby room and beaten by the officers and a few jailers. I heard the man cry out in pain and the profane responses of the officers. The man was dragged by his heels up a flight of cement stairs and deposited inside a cellblock. The next day he required medical attention for head injuries; his body was covered with bruises. Nothing happened to the staff as a result of this incident. It was not an isolated case of beating an inmate or accused person.

There were plenty of other examples of malfeasance and misconduct by staff and administration within that jail and there is no need to post them all here. I called a local newspaper and, with a guarantee of anonymity, met for an interview. I still recall the two of us seated on a park bench by a river as I emptied the bag, so to speak, about what was happening in the jail and some questionable practices by the road deputies, such as stealing from burglary crime scenes. The short version is that it triggered a lengthy investigation by the State Bureau of Investigation. The state press ran with the story of custodial convenience gone wild and "rogue deputies". A grand jury was convened in which all employees were called to testify. A new jail was eventually constructed to replace the old facility. The sheriff and warden are long since deceased. What happened in that jail was neither legal nor right and I am glad to have been a catalyst for change and pleased to finally be able to reveal myself as the whistleblower. I left that job after the grand jury hearings ostensibly to attend graduate school in Atlanta. However, threats of retribution by some of the witch-hunting staff once the anonymous "snitch" was found served as an extra incentive to leave. No hero here. I am sure, in hindsight, I should have done more and earlier during my brief stint with that sheriff's department to report the unconstitutional and unethical practices.

# Incarcerated Female Offenders

> *"I found relief in pills. I had to have the pills to feel normal, to escape the bad feelings. When the doctors' prescriptions did not meet my body's demands, I felt desperate. I robbed drugstores about every three months or two years. I felt trapped."*

> Georgia, No. 9

To close out this this chapter it seems appropriate to mention female offenders, the forgotten ones of criminal justice. In 2013, an estimated 111, 287 women were prisoners housed in a federal or state facility. The top three states for locking up females are Texas (13,830), Florida (7,271), and California (6,297). Texas and Florida have a history of being long on punishment and short on care for defendants. Florida, like Texas, is a grand buffet of neurotic residents and judicial corruption. (Note to self – avoid the sun soaked beaches of wrinklies and Jesus Jumpers in Florida as I contemplate my next crime.).

In 2005 I conducted a study of female criminals in Wisconsin. Rather than focus on the current, dominant explanations touted by feminists as to why females did the nastiness of crime and deviance ("men made us do it!"), I applied for permission to interview 60 of the most dangerous inmates at Taycheedah Correctional Institution in Oshkosh,

Wisconsin. For several months I met with these inmates aka the "N of 60" with N being the sum total of my sample. Intentionally, I avoided all of the current crime statistics on females. My goal was to generate a small nucleus of data and compare it later to what others found. My lengthy, recorded conversations with these women were transcribed and added to my knowledge taken from their case files. The questions sets were two tiered. Level 1 dealt with core information such as prior criminal history, marital status, education, and so forth. Level 2 was a series of open-ended questions that I used to try to gain more insights into the nature of their behavior. Things like "why" mattered more to me than the hard facts about these women. The results were released to the press "Crossing the Gender Gap: Female Offenders in Wisconsin" and presented at a few professional conferences.

Here, for the last time, is my final iteration of that field study. Wisconsin, in 2013, by the way had about 1,239 inmates. It still ranks about midway among all 50 states in the number of incarcerated females. My hunch is that the portrait of the Wisconsin female offender is typical for all other states.

The traits of the N of 60 may still be as useful today:

- 70% are repeat offenders.
- 34% have a GED.
- 50% are unskilled.
- 56% claimed to have done other serious crimes but not caught.
- 53% said they were not abused as a child.

- 79% have at least one child but 60% were never married.
- 60% are white (Wisconsin is a vanilla state)
- 69% admitted to drug and alcohol abuse

Their crimes: murder, crimes against children, escapes, assault and battery, forgery, illegal disposal of a corpse, hanging, theft, parole violations, bank robbery, identity theft, and drug trafficking. This is a partial picture, however, of what these 60 felons had to offer. The open questions elicited more useful remarks.

Q: What type of man are you attracted to (if any)?
A: Bad boys with a dangerous edge to them.

Q: If you love your children and your freedom, why break the law?
A: Not one of the sixty inmates could clearly answer this question.

Q: What effects has your incarceration had on your children?
A: Long list of effects, all bad, varying from attempted suicides, gang life and nervous breakdowns.

Q: Have you ever abused a man?
A: 55% said yes – "he had it coming."

Q: Why did you do it (commit the crime)?

A: 25 different answers and counting. Revenge, addiction, conspiracy, accidental, low self-esteem, and my favorite – "I did it because I loved him/her." I refer the reader back to Chapter 4 for connections to these answers.

The single most important take away from my research was the simplest piece. Most of the incarcerated females were mothers with marginal skills and education. The fathers of their children were "no shows." The offspring struggled to live without their mother. Many failed and ended up in the care of corrections in the State of Wisconsin. I suspect this is the same outcome in all states and there is clearly much to be learned with that simple fact. Is this, in other words, the best we can do with female inmates?

# Maxim

The dreary repetitive nature of corrections is not going to change. There is little creativity in our public response to rehabilitating offenders because, quite honestly, we sit back smugly assured that those people are damned forever. "Can't be fixed Madge." This is not an apology for those who commit crimes against our persons e.g. assault, rape, etc. Nor do I excuse the long line of embittered, soulless characters that cannot live peacefully among us. Truth be told, I support the death penalty for certifiably guilty murderers who have no excuse or mitigating factors on their sides. In those instances, the death sentence is the only appropriate penalty I can think of that is proportionate and deserving for an irreparable crime. It specifically deters the offender from ever killing again, either other inmates or prison staff. Natural law is my guide in this situation. But for most other types of offenders, well, perhaps we need to discuss some more practical, radical penalties aside from simply stealing years from their lives. That may be enough punishment in itself but I believe that more radical interventions and forms of behavior modification may be of more use for repeat offenders.

Jails and prisons are essentially warehouses with small loading docks. Billions of dollars are spent annually on a punishment scheme that does not work in preventing future crimes nor does this approach make society much significantly safer in the long run. It does keep the "bad guys" in specific locations where they may choose to engage in prison / jail crimes to while away the lazy hours e.g. bribing staff, drug trafficking, rapes, and so forth. They have, in other words, transferred their criminal ways to a more structured setting. We deny them access to free society because many of them have proven incapable of living peacefully among us. Others need and deserve another chance outside prison but few will succeed. These inmates emerge from prison (and jails) older and repentant (hopefully) wiser. The barriers to their success, however, are on par with me winning the Kentucky Derby, highly unlikely unless all of the other horses drop dead at the starting gate...

## Looking Elsewhere

http://www.pewtrusts.org/~/media/legacy/uploadedfiles/
wwwpewtrustsorg/reports/sentencing_and_corrections/
StateRecidivismRevolvingDoorAmericaPrisons20pdf.pdf

http://www.theatlantic.com/features/archive/2014/09/
how-gangs-took-over-prisons/379330/

http://www.americanjail.org/10-facts-about-women-in-jails/

http://thefederalist.com/2015/03/04/not-content-with-enor-
mous-taxpayer-subsidies-elon-musk-turned-to-prison-labor-
for-cost-savings/

http://www.bop.gov/

http://www.sentencingproject.org/template/page.cfm?id=92

http://www.mintpressnews.com/obama-administration-
secured-526-months-prison-time-whistleblowers/197755/

# Nine

JUVENILE JUSTICE

*"Please Sir, I Want Some More."*
*"It is easier to build strong children
than to repair broken men."*

FREDERICK DOUGLASS

Any synopsis of juveniles and justice is wrought with haz-ards. The legacy of juvenile justice in America is simply disastrous. For the past 250 years or so society has gradu-ally developed a number of processes, laws, and standards for "handling" juvenile offenders. That same society has also experimented, as the middle and upper class are wont to do, with the minds, bodies and spirits of children, taking many of them to the brink of madness, slavery, and death. The idea that many of these youths have traditionally sprung from the sweaty loins of the lower class and minority groups is no accident. Most crimes do not originate with the gritty underclass. That is a myth promulgated by the rule makers of society. Believe that myth and we are far less likely to pay much attention to the deviance of the rule makers. Crime, as we discussed in previous chapters, happens at all levels of society by all of us. A fairly convincing argument can be made, in fact, that the crimes of the powerful and rich (and clever) have the potential to cause magnified and widespread harm e.g. 2008 collapse of the housing mortgage industry due to wholesale, intentional manipulation and corruption of the marketplace. Millions of people entered foreclosure on their homes or found their sole asset (home) devalued with underwater mortgages. The annual, collective losses due to property crimes by juveniles pale in comparison to the losses incurred by white-collar adult offenders (people and companies) and organized crime.

How does this rant apply to underage offenders? Not much except to remind us that those in charge make the rules, especially in regards to children. The first juvenile court started in 1899 in Chicago. The prevailing philosophy of the juvenile justice system, its raison d'etre, is known as Parens Patriae or "Parent to the country (read=child)". The local government is supposed to identify what is in "the best interests" of the child in distress or in need or just being a delinquent / offender. Therein we find the crux of the problem. How does one define "best interests?" It is a problem that has dogged the juvenile justice system and all of its service branches such as foster care, diversion, therapy programs, and so on. Whose best interests do we adopt and why are they the correct interests or standards? Whose agenda is being served with Parens Patriae?

The "children" of Parens Patriae are among the weakest of society's members. In terms of value and basic human rights, children have historically been treated about as well as we have treated the mentally ill, disabled, and homeless people, which is to say – shabbily and with an emphasis on instilling middle class values on the groups under review. There are those who view these needy groups, including children, as anchors on society, dragging the "normal" classes ever so slowly with the tide but never fast enough. Keep in mind that nursery rhymes and fairy tales were used historically by cultures to terrorize children into submission e.g. boogey men, witches, and demons, or recited as part of a human sacrifice involving some unlucky kids.

Dismiss those ridiculous myths about doe-eyed children being saved from the poor house or death by cholera by a soft-hearted relative with a twinkle in his eye and a hefty bank account (read=buying one's way into the upper class). Dickens' Oliver Twist, for instance, is about the horrors of apprenticeships for children shuttled off to whaling ships, coals mines, brothels, funeral homes, and hat making shops where the mercury used to cure the hats was absorbed into the skin and caused children (and adults) to erupt into violence e.g. "mad as a hatter." The treatment of children has not exactly been roses and champagne for those unlucky enough to fall into the jurisdiction of the courts. It is one of the great and awful examples of mass hubris; the idea that only the ruling social structure can and should inflict its ethics and beliefs (usually based on a religious viewpoint) upon the "needy" (read=different from us). Anything else is seen, as, well, "unreliable" and deficient.

One example of this mentality involved wholesale relocation and adoption of street children. The upper classes introduced a number of remedies to help delinquents and unwanted children. The Orphan Trains (1854-1929), for example, placed roughly 200,000 children from the eastern cities for adoption with rural mid-western farm families. A percentage was used as free labor, some were sexually exploited, others ran away, and some committed suicide.

> *"Thousands are the children of poor foreigners who have permitted them to grow up without school, education, or religion. All the neglect and bad education and evil example of a poor class tend to form others, who, as they mature, swell the ranks of ruffians and criminals. So, at length, a great multitude of ignorant, untrained, passionate, irreligious boys and young men are formed who become the 'dangerous class' in their city."*
>
> Charles Loring Brace

Social tinkering with the welfare of juveniles is a recurrent theme in criminal justice. In juvenile facilities across the country, for instance, sedating or drugging into a state of stupor the underage residents also became a standard practice while in other places sexual abuse (and covered up murders) of juveniles were reported.

> *"The primary predators are adult staff at correctional facilities, not other youth offenders."*

http://www.takepart.com/article/2013/06/10/doj-study-juvenile-justice-sexual-assault

Eventually, in America, a separate system for treating juveniles developed, triggered in part by the example of the first juvenile court with proceedings different from those found in adult court. That was a good first step. Keep juvenile offenders away from hardened adult criminals. At that stage (1899) the idea of Parens Patriae was about to reach its stride within the juvenile courts.

But - let us not enter this issue with eyes shut to some fundamental facts about juvenile offenders:

- There is an estimated 74,181,500 persons under the age of 18 (juveniles).
- 1.4 million juveniles were arrested in 2011. Juvenile arrests for violent crimes disproportionately involved black juveniles. About 51% of all juvenile arrests for violent crimes in 2011 involved black youth and 47% involved white youth.
- Violent crime arrest rates for juveniles declined each of the past 3 years.

- The overall juvenile arrest rate was 38% lower in 2012 than in 1980.
- Juveniles were far less likely to be arrested for <u>property crimes</u> in 2012 than they were 30 years earlier.

http://www.ojjdp.gov/pubs/244476.pdf

The juvenile justice system in existence today is comparable to that of the adult system. Different terms and rights are available to juveniles but the basic process of "disposition" involves finding an outcome or resolution to the needs of the child balanced against the interests of society. Parens Patriae rules all in the juvenile justice system. Juvenile offenders, as the above figures reflect, are the rising generation of criminals. As such, hope remains that some type and level of interdiction will reroute them away from further deviance. Six categories or labels are used to identify juveniles: delinquent, undisciplined, abused, neglected, dependent, and status offenders. The latter is very problematic. It refers to behavior which, if committed by an adult, would not be a crime e.g. running away. The practical age at which juveniles are held responsible for adult crimes varies from state to state. Historically, society has linked puberty (age 12 or 13) as a benchmark for holding a child criminally liable. However, it is assumed that children under the age of seven may never form criminal intent and be prosecuted. After age seven it becomes a crap shoot depending on the mood of the prosecutor guided by state law regarding age of majority, and the type of crime. Then again, take a peek at these vignettes and decide for yourself at what age the juveniles should be held accountable:

*http://www.newser.com/tag/32137/1/juvenile-crime.html*

The majority of juvenile offenders or kids who fall into one or more of the six categories are diverted by police to juvenile court in about 80% of the contacts. In 2013 over one million delinquency cases were disposed of by state juvenile courts. On any given day the headcount of youths in institutions is around 54,000. The turnstile for the juvenile justice system is known as intake. During intake a number of big decisions are made about what to do with a juvenile. The options include sending him/her home to family, foster care placement, medical exams, short-term placement in a facility or halfway house, emergency care, psychiatric review, sending or transferring the case to adult court for further processing, and so forth.

This leads to one essential point, actually it is the reason I have even included juvenile justice in this guidebook. That is, we know for an empirical fact that:

> *"The odds of failure with a juvenile increase significantly the longer we keep and process him/her through the juvenile justice system."*

Exposure to the system, its practices, polices, expectations, is kryptonite to many juveniles. Thus we continue to experiment with alternatives – wagon trains, wilderness camps, self-esteem programs, co-ed living in a secure facility, horse training programs, anti-bullying programs – in the hopes of fitting the square peg in a round hole. The results of these approaches are mixed. Boot camps, for example, use a military regimen of supervision, discipline and physical exercise to effect change in low-risk delinquents. There is no empirical evidence that it works except it does make the residents more physically fit and harder to catch if they run away. Most states have a dead-end facility, usually in a rural setting with a vague holistic title e.g. "Evergreen Restorative School for Challenged Youth" or some such dribble. Behind the manicured exterior landscape you will find fences, large open areas (to spot runners), cameras, staff guards, and very high levels of interior security. This facility will not be public knowledge but they do exist. It is the place of single-cell occupancy and closely monitored behavior.

This, like a sumo wrestler attempting to pole vault, is not a case where much success is expected (or required). The residents are youths who have been repeatedly cycled through other state facilities but to no good effect. These forgotten kids are going nowhere. Security and safety are paramount because the residents are dangerous to themselves and others. In other words, ignore the pleasant sign out front. Behind the sign is a facility that houses the most disturbed juvenile offenders the system has to offer. They are all on their way to adulthood and eventual release. As for how they came to be socio/psychopaths is anybody's guess. The one thread that ties so many issues together in juvenile justice is family. Assuming criminal behavior is not genetically linked (which it could be in some instances) it is fair to ask – where are children most at risk of being victims? The answers are not pretty.

- Children are most likely to be physically hurt at home (first) and at school. At home, mothers are the most common offenders with injuries ranging from temporary bruising to torture and homicide. By far families are the principle destroyers of children.
- (2010) Children in larger families have greater risk of physical and emotional abuse and neglect. Children in rural counties are at greater risk of neglect 33.1 per 1,000).
- One child in every 25 in the United States is abused or neglected. In 2010, child protective services agencies received about 63,500 maltreatment referrals weekly.
- Youth in both the child welfare and juvenile justice systems were found to have worse outcomes than other youth.
- In 2011, about 1 in 5 students reported having been bullied at school and 1 in 6 reported having been cyberbullied.
- Nationwide, 20% of high school students said they were bullied at school in 2011
- On average, between 2001 and 2010, about 1,600 juveniles were murdered annually in the U.S. Nearly half (49%) of juvenile murder victims in 2010 were black, 47% were white

- Between 1980 and 2010, 4 of every 5 murder victims ages 15–17 were killed with a firearm. Persons ages 7–17 are about as likely to be victims of suicide as they are to be victims of homicide.

http://www.ncjj.org/nr2014/index.html

# Maxim

Sadly, the most dangerous places on earth for children are those places where they should be the safest. Instead, families continue to intentionally injure and murder their offspring with depressing regularity including this very important fact: "Most victims of child maltreatment are <u>white</u>." In 2010, most victims of child maltreatment were white (44.8%), followed by black (21.9%) and Hispanic (21.4%).

http://www.ncjj.org/nr2014/index.html

Let's not tiptoe softly away from that fact too quickly. White families, not black or brown, neglect and mistreated their offspring at a greater frequency. It is white mothers who are to be feared as the more probable Shivas of Destruction of their kids. Also, it is no secret that families without employment are more likely to take their angst out on the weakest members. And, to complete the trifecta, children without an education are going to be locked into the bottom tier of the social caste system of capitalism. They will absolutely mimic as adults, the destructive behaviors, language, and values practiced upon them as children.

Schools are not much safer. Schools are the place where a child's mind is opened to knowledge but it comes at a prohibitive cost; School can become a minefield for many children who endure violent assaults, bullying (direct and online), threats, and thefts at the hands of predator students and, occasionally, staff. Joined with the realization that illiterate, incapable parents produce equally unprepared children, it is no surprise that violence in the home is reflected within school settings by pupils who cannot resolve their problems peacefully.

*"School Violence Leads to 90,000-Plus Emergency-Room Trips a Year, Says Study."*

http://blogs.edweek.org/edweek/rulesforengagement/2014/01/school_violence_leads_to_er_trips_for_more_than_90000_a_year_study_finds.html

The juvenile justice system is meant to serve as a benevolent parent who, ironically, can end up doing more harm than good. There is a point of no return when a hardened juvenile is lost to society. Some end up in that facility of last resort noted above. Others, well, a few flourish but many become adult predators, full-time victims, or occupy a pauper's grave somewhere. I spent 10 years conducting detailed field research into the sexual trafficking of children in the United States, along with my gifted colleague Donald Poffenberger. Our work intersected all three settings routinely. We discovered no miracle cures for juvenile justice or the ongoing victimization of children. It certainly seems like the time is at hand to progress beyond the status quo, for society and government to interrupt the cycle of delinquency by addressing the welfare of children with creative, practical remedies rather than rhetoric, well wishes and prayers.

## Looking Elsewhere

The Sexual Trafficking in Children: An Investigation of the Child Sex Trade; Daniel S. Campagna and Donald Poffenberger, 1986.

Juvenile Offenders and Victims: 2014 National Report; Melissa Sickmund and Charles Puzzanchera, Editors, National Center for Juvenile Justice, December 2014

# Ten

## BREATHTAKINGLY AWFUL: THE CRIMES OF THE VERY NASTY

*"These dwell among the blackest souls,*
*loaded down deep by sins of differing types.*
*If you sink far enough, you'll see them all."*

DANTE ALIGHIERI, *INFERNO*

It should be apparent by now, amidst the swirl and clouds of statistics, that crime is frequent in America and is limited only by our imaginations and innate creativity to be deviant, however one defines it. In a nation of 300 million people perhaps it is inevitable that the daily news reports should read like something out of Dante's Inferno. It is a marketplace where let civis cavete or "let the citizen beware" is the rule of life (and death). We hope that the odds of being seriously victimized are unlikely, of mega-lottery proportions so that life remains a fairly predictable series of right step, left step, repeat for a fixed number of decades and we shuffle off to a hole in the ground or somewhere without income tax. The odds, by the way, of not being victimized are slim. Some scholars claim that every adult will be the victim of a serious crime (felony) two or three times in a lifetime. Methods for reducing those odds significantly exist but, with few exceptions, people act with convenience in mind first and safety second. Besides, most of us, you may recall from Chapter 3, cross back and forth across the bipolar spectrum of being a criminal and being a victim.

But this is supposed to be a guidebook of sorts. Something like a tourist's package to an eco-tour of a third-world country ("Oh Sal, how do these people live in such squalor??? It's disgusting! Keep your hands on your wallet.") and as such there are some special crimes worth entering in one's consciousness. As a reminder that from the womb to our last gasp, we are rarely free of criminal endeavors, I offer this set of snapshots of four types of deviance that embrace several key icons of society: health care, religion, death care, and capitalism.

### Snapshot 1: The Human Body & Mind Repair Shop

*"It should seem a strange principle to enumerate as the very first requirement in a hospital that it should do the sick no harm."*

Florence Nightingale

An impressive array of felonies and misdemeanors occur in those facilities constructed and designed to repair the human body and mind. I refer to the medical and health care industries, including hospitals, nursing homes of various types, psychiatric and dental facilities, private clinics, and so forth. Unless you practice caveat emptor (buyer beware) and have a touch of natural suspicion about those who assume care over our minds and bodies, you will probably not notice these crimes. They involve violations of the processes, standards of conduct and procedures by the employees of those institutions; some of the acts are accidental in nature or done without mens rea (criminal intent). Each variant of the Human Body Repair & Mind Shop (HBRMS) is regulated, however poorly, by a professional association that routinely circles the malpractice wagons when claims are made by patients about malfeasance and misconduct.

In fact, so closely knit are these respective professions that the following statistics are very crude underestimates. The professions are very unwilling to maintain accurate records of crimes and abuses in their work and even less willing to make such misconduct known to the public (bad for business and the accused worked so hard to get a license). Reliable data about crimes such as drug abuse by nurses and other staff, sexual assaults of mentally ill patients, the total headcount of falsified filings for roots canals and other oral surgeries by dentists, and kickbacks from the pharmaceutical companies to doctors who push high risk drugs on some patients, is not easily acquired. Often the acts are reclassified as something other crimes or couched in more "palatable" terms to avoid the implication of wrongdoing. That fact, in itself, should sound an alarm bell or two in the consumer as explained in the following narrative:

Top 10 prescription medication drugs abused by medical providers

"There are three categories of medications that health care providers tend to abuse: sedatives, opiates and benzodiazepines. Following is a detailed description of medications most likely to be abused by medical staff. But first, we provide an alphabetic list of the brand names for particular drugs used most by medical workers."

1. Ativan
2. Demerol
3. Dilaudid
4. Diprovan (Propofol)
5. Fentanyl
6. Morphine
7. OxyContin
8. Percocet
9. Vicodin
10. Xanax

http://prescription-drug.addictionblog.org/top-10-prescription-drugs-medical-professionals-use-or-abuse/

This particular article identifies which drugs and their side effects are most often used by health care workers while on duty. Moreover, the idea that these drug abusers need "help" rather than face criminal charges or loss of license is a recurrent theme in the health care industry. This is curious. If a street offender breaks into a pharmacy to steal drugs and is caught, prosecution, not "help" is inevitable. If a nurse or doctor steals Xanax or Morphine from a hospital drug supply, she/he needs "help." Why do we view employees treating our minds and bodies while under the influence of various drugs that affect their minds and bodies as "needful" persons rather than criminals? What is the difference?

> *"A USA TODAY review shows more than 100,000 doctors, nurses, medical technicians and health care aides are abusing or dependent on prescription drugs in a given year, putting patients at risk."*

http://www.usatoday.com/story/news/nation/2014/04/15/doctors-addicted-drugs-health-care-diversion/7588401/

The war on drugs is not expansive enough; it should include the abuse, consumption, and trafficking (and addictions) of prescription drugs, theft and use by health care workers of stock supply, addictions by surgeons and staff, the role of pharmaceutical firms in touting drugs with high rates of harm to patients, criminal inquiries into the theft of patient medications, and overdoses.

> *"Across the country, 44,000 people died from drug overdoses in 2013, more than double the number in 1999,*

*the study by the non-profit group, Trust for America's Health found. Nearly 52 percent of the deaths were related to prescription drugs."*

https://www.yahoo.com/health/deaths-from-drug-overdoses-rise-across-america-121757195727.html

Drug abuse by those in the health care industry is not new but, from the patient's perspective, it is certainly dangerous and worrisome. Self-medicated physicians and nurses do not inspire confidence in their job performance. It remains a problem infrequently addressed within the confines of the facility. Drug abuse is not the exclusive crime of the medical care professions. Theft, robbery, assaults, murder, and other major crimes against patients occur in a number of health care settings. Some facilities inadvertently hire "Angels of Death", nurses who kill patients by the score for various reasons. In nursing homes, where life expectancies are limited, the problem of crime and institutional neglect is exacerbated:

*"More than 30% of all nursing homes experience some form of resident abuse: Nearly 1/3 of all nursing homes have residents that are subject to abuse, whether it's by staff or other residents. These include malnutrition, physical abuse, psychological distress, exploitation, neglect, and sexual abuse."*

http://www.nursinghomesabuseblog.com/nursing-home-abuse/nursing-home-abuse-disturbing-statistics-on-patient-care/

Although patients and family need, for understandable reasons, to believe in the myth of the Hippocratic Oath and the innate promise of safe, therapeutic care, the realities can be very different. At one corporate nursing home, for example, a tag team of doctors would stop by every day or two to briefly check and initial the clipboard for a patient, ask a question or two (optional), and exit. Room to room these healers went and each visit was another billable moment added to the patient's monthly bill which accrued to the thousands of dollars. At another (state) nursing home, the valuables of sleeping patients were stolen by staff upon entry. There are certainly very skilled, responsible health care workers BUT the Cheesecake Theory of Crime is, in my opinion, still as pertinent in the medical industry as anywhere else. The reader may recognize that the victims are invariably seen as targets of special vulnerability; these are patients who, simply stated, put their trust in the wrong people. When temptation and opportunity arise for some of these personnel, not much good for the patient (or government) results:

> *"Since 2007, as part of increased efforts to tackle Medicare fraud, federal authorities have charged nearly 2,100 people with falsely billing the Medicare program more than $6.5 billion, according to the Justice Dept. Thursday's arrests bring that total to over 2,300 people who have billed over $7 billion."*

http://news.yahoo.com/243-people-arrested-712-million-medicare-fraud-doj-152307574.html

## Snapshot 2: Crimes of Religion; "Forgive me Father, Allah, Yahweh…, for I Have Sinned."

*"All religion, my friend, is simply evolved out of fraud, fear, greed, imagination, and poetry."*

Edgar Allan Poe

There is something inherently repugnant about the moral contradictions found in the crimes of religions and their spiritual icons. Everyday throughout the world the faithful followers of some supernatural entity kneel / stand in a church or stand before the Wailing Wall or unroll a prayer rug in a mosque and chant their mantras of forgiveness and love. I am a pragmatist when it comes to supernatural and mythological beings but even more so when it concerns their earthly representatives, the preachers, imams, ministers, priests and other after-life coaches holding open the portals to the Big Jump into infinity. If you need that balm, good for you. I say that, not as a sarcastic remark, but as a reminder that crimes by religious leaders and employees do not negate our constitutional rights to due process and protection. Besides, you doubtless noticed, almost all of these religious ideologies include themes of intolerance aimed at hurting or exploiting some other group or people, especially women and children and the "unfaithful" which I guess means me and probably my Uncle Phil in his ice cream truck.

*"If Only There Was Somewhere He Could Have Turned for Moral Guidance: Suspended Catholic Monsignor*

*Kevin Wallin, 63, was sentenced in May to more than five years in prison for running a meth distribution ring from Bridgeport, Connecticut, where he also operated a sex shop to launder the drug profits. (Though he faced a 10-year sentence, he had a history of charity work and submitted more than 80 letters of support from high-ranking clergy.)"*

*Associated Press via WTIC-TV (Hartford), 5-7-2015*

So, my investigative curiosity is drawn to those leaders who claim to know the mind and intent of an omnipotent deity. These leaders are, after all, human beings prone to the weaknesses of the flesh and spirit. Or are they? Do these people commit acts of mala in se and mala prohibita? Do Mormon women wear special underwear (pink thongs?) – wait, that image has caused male cramping in my lower places. Move on. The answer, obviously, certainly is yes. Hell yes! And square that number by 666. The odd fact is that too many congregations forgive those crimes, mostly, but I am not sure what their Gods would say about that level of hypocrisy.

It is estimated, for example, that upwards of several thousand clergy have been found guilty or accused of sexual misconduct during the past decades since any useful data (1960's) was first made available. Take a look at the available figures of accused clerics whose names have been made public.

| 24 | Bishops |
|---|---|
| 3,536 | Priests |
| 91 | Nuns |
| 245 | Brothers |
| 56 | Deacons |
| 27 | Seminarians |
| 3,973 | Total |

http://www.bishop-accountability.org/AtAGlance/data.htm

From 1950 – 2013 (no data available by the Catholic church for 2003), 6,427 clerics were accused of sexual crimes, nineteen of whom were bishops. The names of all of these clerics have not been made public and the physical location of these persons is kept secret by the church. A reported 17,259 survivors have been identified for that time period. Less than 2% (83) of the allegations were false. 3,000 civil lawsuits filed between 1984-2009 resulted in roughly $2 billion in awards.

http://www.bishop-accountability.org/usccb/implementation/report_on_2013.pdf

Please note that this is widely considered to be a conservative estimate. Pope Benedict, for instance, has defrocked 400 priests for child sex abuse during the past two years.

http://www.truecrimereport.com/bad_clergy/

Okay, I can hear you saying that nuns are exempt from this this sort of behavior. These little darlings of mercy and care would not violate the trust of their wards, children, other nuns, and the elderly. Au contraire, mon cher. If we dig deep into the online case logs of incidents regarding abuses and crimes by nuns, it is clear that even God's Angels on Earth are prone sometimes to diddle and fiddle with deviance:

http://www.snapnetwork.org/nun_abuse.

After all, we are discussing human beings with virtues and warts some of whom harbor very twisted, repressed sexual desires. As one nun told me with a grin while flashing a silver wedding band – "I am married to the big guy!" My first thought – "Is that nunspeak for something creepy?" But, that's just me being a cynic. I see celibacy as a deeply unnatural state that attempts to deny a primal biological urge of the species to procreate (and have fun). There is nothing "natural" or divine about celibacy unless someone has lost his/her sexual mojo, is ill, etc. but without sex there is no species. Consequently, I suspect nuns are no different from other clergy in their secret hankerings and misdeeds:

> *"Former residents of the Catholic Nazareth order's homes say they suffered appalling, systematic cruelty."*

http://www.independent.co.uk/news/nuns-abused-hundreds-of-children-1171988.html

As for other religions, it should be no surprise that crimes by their clergy and lay staff are not made public by the church, synagogue, temple, etc. unless the victim(s) files a criminal complaint. Nor are accurate records faithfully (no pun meant) kept by religious groups of such behavior. Reliable, effective oversight of crimes committed by clergy simply does not exist, regardless of the lukewarm efforts of the media to keep us posted. Typically, it is the victims who collate hard facts about these crimes and try to register their findings with the criminal justice system and in online formats. Otherwise, we hit the proverbial stonewall of silence by religions. "Don't know, don't want to know" should be their motto and perhaps a rallying cry for their congregations. Sometimes, the leaders of these religious organizations out themselves by wild and crazy behavior with prostitutes, drugs, sexual acts with minors (statutory rape), homosexual acts, embezzlement, and financial misconduct that bankrupts the non-profit entity. You know, the sort of behavior that a god would frown upon...

> "*Southern Baptist churches are rarely the first party to report allegations of child sexual abuse by clergy to legal authorities, according to an analysis of news stories aggregated at a website maintained by an advocate for victims.*"

https://baptistnews.com/archives/item/6956-news-analysis-churches-not-typically-first-reporters-of-sexual-abuse#sthash.3BLOsrcY.dpuf

To wrap up this brief snapshot on religious crimes, it is worth noting that no mention has been made of crimes committed by the institutions of organized religion such as covering up knowledge of a crime, acts against humanity (enslavement of women and children), genocide, fiscal improprieties, and so forth. That is also a long list and the subject of someone else's book someday!

There remains, however, one idea that continually nags me about the "faithful" memberships of religions whose clergy and lay staff have broken the law, especially those involving sex acts with children. To those kneeling worshippers I cannot help but wonder – how do one justify giving one's spiritual loyalty and support to a church / religion that covers up its misdeeds at the expense of children? Are we saying that one's need to be part of the spiritual membership and believe in a supernatural being outweigh the basic rights of a child? Help me to understand. I spent ten years meeting countless numbers of children who were sexually victimized. I do not recall a single one of them who could reconcile the harm done to them with the notion of "It is God's will."

How do people live with that? Try to imagine the screams and terror of these young victims as they are anally sodomized and repeatedly victimized by religious leaders or staff? 17,259 underage victims of sexual abuse by clergy have been identified thus far. We must accept that this number is just the tip of an enormous iceberg, regardless of which organized religion we discuss. Why not take a different tack and act on moral principles far greater than any spiritual duties? Get off your knees from the pews and prayer rugs, stand up and advocate for the victims.

You must also realize that, with your silence and unresponsiveness, you may be viewed as indirectly complicit in those terrible crimes. You know, as co-conspirators which is something I encountered hundreds of times in my research into sexually dysfunctional (read=PFU=Profoundly Fucked Up) children and their families. Indifference and silence, in the case of congregations, are the two easiest ways to assure that such crimes continue. Some might argue that only cowards would fail to demand accountability from their religious trailblazers, those hoodoo voodoo chiefs who perform that sleight of hand known as the grand illusion of faith reflected in the remark – "Forgive me for my transgressions." I hope all congregations stop waiting for a spinal donor to show up and provide them with the backbones to stand up for the victims. In short, demand accountability from the people who provide you spiritual succour.

http://www.stopbaptistpredators.org/index.htm

## Snapshot 3: "Where's Grandma's Gold Teeth?" Morgues and Funeral Homes

You would think and expect that, once dead, our bodies would be treated with some degree of respect, that all of our troubles and worries will vanish, and afterlife harmony will reign. Not necessarily. The fact is that every year a number of very nasty crimes happen from our arrival in a morgue to a funeral home of choice:

https://www.fbi.gov/news/stories/2010/september/funeral-scams).

These crimes involve dead people, grandparents and children and moms and dads and anyone else not breathing. You know, the cadavers, the folks we mourn for and try to honor with parting rituals. Except there are people and companies that simply cannot resist tampering with our mortal clay remains for profit and pleasure one last time.

The National Funeral Home Directors Association (http://nfda.org/index.php/about-funeral-service-/trends-and-statistics.html) is the mouthpiece for the industry. It is also one of less reliable sources for information on crimes committed by and within funeral homes. These crimes include stealing gold and silver fillings (and jewelry) from a cadaver, failure to properly dispose of human remains, bait and switch practices with caskets and cemetery plots, insurance scams, overcharging and double billing for services, necrophilia (mala in se acts), taking and posting photos of cadavers online (selfies, god love 'em one and all!) and maybe chuck in some high impact cardio exercise through grave robbing (just an afterthought to stopping by the gym?).

*"ROME, Ga. — The families of more than 300 people whose bodies were found strewn across the grounds of a Georgia crematory will receive nearly $40 million in a settlement announced Thursday with the business and 58 funeral homes across the South."*

http://articles.latimes.com/2004/mar/12/nation/na-crematory12

# The Cheesecake Theory of Crime

*"Lancaster County District Attorney Craig Stedman announced at a Friday press conference that Benjamin M. Siar Jr., operator of the Gundel Funeral Home, would be charged with four counts of abuse of a corpse, and four counts of theft by deception, for accepting money for cremation services that were never performed."*

http://lancasteronline.com/news/funeral-director-benjamin-siar-jr-charged-with-abuse-of-corpses/article_d626ac53-e2e3-59ca-9e14-c1b6ab9dcbd8.html

Crimes involving abuse of the dead, assuming they are not zombies, are vile and an utter disregard of the trauma endured by families. Does the deceased continue to have constitutional rights? Hmm...not so much. Without an advocate or honest service provider, a corpse is deposable detritus. Of course, in a truly efficient capitalist system, nothing should be wasted when it comes to revenue streams. I suggest we stuff and embalm family members. Put them upright in vacuum sealed glass "phone booths" and charge admission to view the dearly departed. Maybe add some video clips of the deceased when they were having a silly moment? "Here's dad falling off the house while trying to shovel snow off the roof." That would be a hit in Minnesota, eh?

On the flip side, the only way society finds out about nasty acts in morgues and funeral homes are when the crimes are "too obvious" to be ignored:

*"El Paso County sheriff's investigators have arrested three people on suspicion of corpse abuse after finding five bodies, including a fetus, in various stages of decomposition at a Central El Paso funeral home."*

http://www.elpasotimes.com/news/ci_26560814/three-people-arrested-accused-abusing-corpses-at-central

What these types of activities clearly demonstrate is a need for some type of direct supervision of funeral homes and their practices. Unfortunately, it is again a case of buyer beware. I know of various incidents in which valuables left on the deceased were stolen either at the morgue or funeral home(s). Wallets, rings, jewelry, precious metals, teeth, all vanished! Even Houdini and his magical bag of tricks could not compete with the nimble fingers of corpse robbing staff once someone has died. Would, however, that these disgusting behaviors stopped with simple theft:

*"An Ohio morgue attendant admitted to having sex with at least 100 corpses while on the job, federal officials said in court Friday. Kenneth Douglas, a 60-year-old Hamilton, Ohio resident, said he had sex with the corpses between 1976 and 1992 while working the night shift, WCPO reported."*

http://www.huffingtonpost.com/2014/08/18/morgue-attendant-100-sex_n_5687795.html

# The Cheesecake Theory of Crime

That's right folks. For 16 years Mr. Douglas would slide off his work pants as the occasions arose at the morgue and climb atop a female cadaver and insert his erect yin into her flaccid, lifeless yang. Hmm…now what is the right type of mood music for these lopsided romantic interludes? A few aromatic candles and incense? Perhaps some industrial strength cleaner for the mess afterwards? Be assured Mr. Douglas is not the first necrophiliac to work in morgues or graveyards. If there is an afterlife, which is contestable, imagine the perplexed expressions on the ghost faces of those one hundred women. Not a pretty sight. Morgues are evidently unsupervised opportunities for amoral employees to carry out thefts and sexual assaults. I truly wish it was unnecessary to describe these pathetic "underground" behaviors but knowledge sometimes translates into power. 24/7 video monitoring of all cadavers in morgues and funeral homes (and patients) in medical facilities is both practical and eminently doable thus offering a level of protection not presently available to victims. After all, if technology can mass produce cheap cameras to provide an endless, boring stream of videos about how we spend our vacations, why not put them to use, ala CCTV, on behalf of the deceased and patients? It is a start.

The point of this vignette is that, similar to the health care and religious industries of this nation, consumers / citizens must be on guard and advocate for their best interests. In both of these industries the survivors are vulnerable and in a state of high stress. To crooked service providers and offenders, that vulnerability is a chance to prey on us. One of the central themes of this guidebook is that profits can and often do outweigh ethics and lawful conduct. And dying is a very lucrative business in America:

> *"Today the average traditional funeral costs between $8,000 and $10,000, and about 42% of people are cremated. The US funeral industry accounts for about $20 billion in annual economic activity, with around 130,000 employees that make a living on the 1.5 million people that go to rest each year."*

http://www.forbes.com/sites/perianneboring/2014/04/25/the-death-of-the-death-care-industry-and-eternal-life-online/

### Snapshot 4: Crimes of the White Collared Slum Dogs

> *"You've built yourselves a god from silver and gold.*
> *How does that differ from idol worship, except*
> *those people worship one god and you a hundred?"*
> — Dante Alighieri, *Inferno*

I must confess that this final snapshot is too easy. There is so much well documented evidence that my comments are basically a series of highlights. I refer to the crimes of the corporations, their managers, and the uber rich. Cybercrimes are interwoven within these activities because a basic knowledge of code programming / scripting, hacking, identity theft, and scamming are common elements of many white-collar crimes. White collar and cyber crooks have very useful tool chests and knowing how to manipulate the Interweb is a large hammer in that chest. For instance, we know that everyday some clever dick installs a credit card skimming device at your neighborhood gas pumps. Every day, a "financial advisor" knowingly gives false advice to a wealthy client which results in a hefty commission to the advisor. And every day a cyber criminal in Prague or Peking or Des Moines flexes his pudgy little fingers and launches yet another successful break-in of a corporate or public data bank of highly sensitive information:

http://www.privacyrights.org/data-breach

If you decide to read no further in this section I urge you to pause and review the knowledge base provided in the above site. You may be surprised. The cyber criminals are having a field day at the expense of everyone foolish enough to believe that one's identity, personal accounts, medical records, emails, and digital transmission are protected with unencrypted passwords and security software. Just as another side note, deleted information often is stored in latent sectors of one's computer. Not visible but present nonetheless. As of July 1, 2105, the estimated number of security breaches ranges from 200-250 million names and accounts including the businesses and organizations that house information about us. This type of activity is so common that only a born again idiot would think their digital information was secure. Think of that information as residing in a safe with a one-number combination for entry.

These particular crimes and deviant acts are legion. Bernard Madoff resides at the Federal Prison in Butner, North Carolina and contemplates (maybe) where it all went wrong. "It" refers to decades of operating the most successful Ponzi Scheme in criminal history, to the tune of about $30 billion dollars in embezzled funds. A Ponzi Scheme occurs when someone offers another person a chance to make very large profits with little risk by investing in a "can't lose" proposition. The schemer must continually ass more investors to pay off partially the previous investors. It is still amazing to me how many and what sort of groups and people flocked to his carnival pitch:

http://s.wsj.net/public/resources/documents/st madoff victims 20081215.html

Yet Madoff, for all of his sins, was simply a benchmark. Compared with other fraudsters, Madoff is symbolic of the diseases of capitalism. Those who argue the virtues of capitalism are those reaping its rewards. The captains of industry, the "entrepreneurs" of free markets and innovations, the cutting edge risk takers of money and technology are sometimes crooks. Capitalism rewards monopolies and the centralization of power (forgive my preaching here) and it is evident within the criminal justice system:

> *"Corporate Compliance Counsel Draws Mixed Reviews, Even State of the Art Programs Can Turn Out to Be Corrupt."*

# The Cheesecake Theory of Crime

http://www.corporatecrimereporter.com/

It seems impossible to sustain a system of justice in which so few people and companies dominate the marketplace of ideas (read= actual and disguised monopolies) and saturate the popular culture with their private agendas. This translates poorly for those dealing with the criminal justice system. That system is based on a set of values and rules found in the U.S. Constitution (general guidelines), laws (specific), community standards, and those with a financial interest in the outcomes. All of these things are directly tied to power expressed as wealth. Not always and not everywhere, certainly, but here's the problem –

> *"Far more worrying is the tendency of the superrich to use their wealth, power, and influence to further their own interests as a class — doing their best to ensure that neither political party does much of anything concrete or specific to diminish that wealth, power, and influence.* That *is the oligarchic aim: To enhance the dominance of the superrich over the American economy and political culture to such an extent that they become effectively untouchable. Not only are they insulated from the meritocratic checks of the market, but also from government oversight and regulation, living lives far above and beyond the rest of us."*
>
> *Damon Linker;* http://theweek.com/articles/ 452173/shameful-selfdealing-americas-superrich

Assigning blame at the doorsteps of the rich, a capitalist system, and a machine bound global society is not enough. What, exactly, are the sort of behaviors and questionable practices associated with these offenders? There is a wide assortment of white-collar crimes. They include a multitude of frauds e.g. bankruptcy, mortgage, money laundering, securities and stock, scams e.g. price fixing, stock (pump and dump), adoption and social security card, and unnecessary repairs. This is a very short list distilled from a very deep tank of wrongdoing. White collar (and cyber) crimes are pervasive and often difficult to prosecute. Civil proceedings with a promise by the offender (person or company) to give restitution are the method by which many of these crimes are settled.

> *"This past year, the Justice Department reached multibillion-dollar settlements with Bank of America and JPMorgan Chase for selling shoddy mortgage-backed securities before the financial crisis hit in 2008. Most of the loans packaged for investors were made by companies acquired by the banks as the real estate market spiraled downward in 2008, so they paid for the sins of others."*

http://dealbook.nytimes.com/2014/12/29/the-year-in-white-collar-crime/?_r=0

The example provided above is one of many in which companies were fined rather than prosecuted for illegal financial dealings. That is the "golden parachute" of capitalism; responsibility for criminal acts will not be expected or pursued aggressively by the criminal justice system. Showcase trials will periodically be announced to alert the public that an ambitious, "get tough" prosecutor is prepared to tackle big business and political corruption. Several years later, the case is quietly disposed of, often with little more than a fine and a warning to not be so goddamn stupid next time. Meanwhile, the prosecutor has moved on to a legislative job, a judgeship, or some such option. For these crimes to continue without interruption so often requires the consent and cooperation of others; legislators with donation ties to companies and political interest groups, judges and prosecutors needing a money injection to get re-elected, and an absentee press. What are not welcome are people who want to put a spotlight on an injustice:

http://www.cracked.com/personal-experiences-1312-5-terrible-things-i-learned-as-corporate-whistleblower.html

As noted elsewhere, white collar and cybercrime is endemic to society. It affects our health (overcharging and inflated insurance premiums), our financial wellbeing (hello stock fraud, mortgage industry bailout), and quality of life (pollution, rights of the accused, likelihood of personal victimization). Or, in the case of children stricken with cancer because of alleged contamination and discharged pollutants caused by a washing machine plant:

*"A lawsuit against Whirlpool Corp. has been settled over contaminated land in northern Ohio near where dozens of children were sickened with cancer."*

http://news.yahoo.com/polluted-land-owners-ohio-end-suit-against-whirlpool-135343183.html

Notice that this case was resolved through a civil action, a lawsuit, and not a criminal hearing. Companies are almost completely immune from prosecution for alleged fatal or serious harm to health incidents caused by their products and services. Whirlpool, in this case, denies any wrongdoing even though thirty-five children, since the 1990's, have coincidentally been diagnosed with cancer in the area close to the plant and three have died. "Nothing to see here, folks, keep moving." This may be the most appropriate motto of white collar crimes.

My rough and biased guess is that losses due to these type of crimes annually rings in at over 1 trillion dollars, more than the combined costs of the war on drugs, gangs, and homeland security, among others. Feel welcome to prove me wrong.

## Maxim

Upon reflection, it seems that the most useful way to distill the various ideas in this chapter is through a personal vignette. At the start of my doctoral studies, about the same time as prime numbers and gunpowder were discovered, I was victimized by a white-collar crook named K. Hancock. He defrauded me of my life savings - $24,000 – in a home purchase deal. Using forged documents and other methods, Mr. Hancock bankrupted me. I was married at the time with a two-year son. We lost everything in one swift maneuver with no other financial resources to fall back upon.

While keeping up with extremely complex coursework I went after Mr. Hancock. In my spare time I hounded him everywhere he went; wife's home, office, girlfriend's residence, and many out-of-state locations. I contacted every conceivable person and agency for help in his apprehension. That list included every state and federal legislator, every Atlanta area media source, the FBI, the Georgia Bureau of Investigation, IRS, prosecutors, consumer advocacy groups, and so on. In the process I stumbled upon a logjam of other victims, close to one hundred I believe, and none had any success using the criminal justice or political systems in bringing Mr. Hancock to heel. But none had gone as far and for as long as I did. The crimes of Hancock crossed multiple jurisdictions and occurred over a two-year period. For a few months, out of desperation to keep on his trail, I did some free-lance bounty hunting for a bail bondsman to whom Mr. Hancock owed a "fail to appear in court" fee. In exchange I gained access to more detailed information as to Hancock's whereabouts. Six months and many miles later, after chasing him from jurisdiction to jurisdiction and persuading judges to file arrest warrants, Mr. Hancock agreed to a settlement with me for $24,000 via an intermediary. Basically Mr. Hancock was fatigued from running away from me and the court warrants for his arrest. I took the money, split it with my ex-wife, and never forgot that, in our time of great need and despair, not a single agent or group of any political, judicial, or governmental entity could or would help us (or the other victims). I was going through a divorce, attending graduate classes, sleeping in the back of a pick-up truck, and trying to recover from walking pneumonia and strep throat. I had to have closure with this swine, if for no other reason than my ex-wife needed the money to help raise our son without financial hardships. I was naïve to believe in the many agencies I visited. Sometimes justice is hand delivered. Plus, I refused to go on through life as one of Hancock's many victims.

Mr. K. Hancock – I never forgot you. And I got you dead to rights... Oh, the peachy swell times you and I shared as the victim pursued the thief. Do you remember me walking into your office that sunny day while your secretary was out? And standing over you demanding my money? And you, a grown man, kneeling on the carpet with tears in your eyes asking for more time. If it were not for the fact that I have a headstrong, fiercely "anti-victim" mindset, this case would never have been resolved, especially not by any agent or group of the criminal justice system. My $24,000 would have been lost forever. This is not braggadocio on my part; it does make me, however, wonder to this day -

*"Exactly whose interests do the police, the courts and the prisons represent?"*

Looking Elsewhere
http://finance.yahoo.com/news/ubs-says-settle-fx-probe-pay-545-million-053323621--sector.html

http://www.bbc.com/future/story/20141027-the-hidden-ways-youre-tracked

http://www.go-gulf.com/blog/cyber-crime/

http://www.pwc.com/en_US/us/increasing-it-effectiveness/publications/assets/2014-us-state-of-cybercrime.pdf

http://www.heritage.org/research/reports/2014/10/cyber-attacks-on-us-companies-in-2014

http://money.cnn.com/2014/08/18/technology/security/hospital-chs-hack/index.html

http://www.mintpressnews.com/obama-administration-secured-526-months-prison-time-whistleblowers/197755/

http://www.wsws.org/en/articles/2014/06/16/mipo-j16.html

# Eleven

*"The end of law is not to abolish or restrain,
but to preserve and enlarge freedom. For in
all the states of created beings capable of law,
where there is no law, there is no freedom."*

JOHN LOCKE

This is the last chapter whereby I tidy up plenty of loose ideas into a cohesive whole. Except it's not going to turn out that way. After 30 plus years of working in many capacities within the discipline and practice of criminal justice I intend to air my dirty linen and say what I believe to be true and provocative. My version of truth challenges the underlying assumptions of organized religions, politics, and corporate theologies like capitalism. My "propositions" are both politically incorrect and unrealistic. Yet the subtheme of this book is irreverence so, much like a three-decker frigate sailing with the wind, I intend to let fly a number of broadsides at a number of sacred ideas. My advice to the reader – duck.

## Awkward Questions

- Why are black males overrepresented in arrest, conviction, and incarceration rates? Either these men are actually committing the lion's share of crime or they are not. Which is it?

*"Baltimore reached a grim milestone on Friday, three months after riots erupted in response to the death of Freddie Gray in police custody: With 45 homicides in July, the city has seen more bloodshed in a single month than it has in 43 years."*

http://news.yahoo.com/baltimore-killings-soar-level-unseen-43-years-184317889.html#

I have heard the familiar mantras of poverty, no jobs, and racial oppression within black communities in such cities as Detroit, MI, St. Louis, MO, New Orleans, LA, and Columbia, SC. I think those explanations matter but they do not tell the whole tale. Giving black males sustainable wages and benefits does not guarantee a reduced level of crime. If nothing else has been shown to be depressingly true – we all commit crimes but we do not all get caught and our race may have little to do with the decision to arrest or not. Suburban communities, for instance, continue to wrestle with the recurring crimes of drug abuse, addiction, underage drinking, sexual crimes, and retail theft by their spawn – educated vanilla, brown, red, pink and plaid children with morose expressions, weekly allowances, and cell phones. Moreover, white collar crooks, the ones who have access to the resources and necessary technology to commit white collar acts, continue to reproduce and make more of these shitty children. Equally revealing, the white collar and cyber offenders are rarely prosecuted and convicted for their sins and most definitely do not share cells with gangbangers and drug dealers.

But, because I enjoy pushing the point, let us assume the mantras about class and race and the link to crime are partially right. They are also partially wrong; shifting blame to the above ideas e.g. poverty and innate traits of racial classes is disingenuous. Let us not disregard completely a number of other politically incorrect explanations that deserve some notice.

- How is it that other minorities have been able to succeed without shipping so many of their offspring to the courts and correctional systems? What do these parents do differently that black parents do not e.g. core values? I often hear media soundbites of black and white church members discussing the influence of their spirituality on curbing criminality by black males. In my opinion, and assuming the statistics are true, that influence is an illusion. It is simply not working. To all of the readers shaking your head in dismay at my remarks, I would remind you that crimes by corporations (price fixing), cyber crimes (hacking), political misconduct (bribery), religions (sexual abuse), and environmental crimes (pollution) cause wholesale damage to all tiers of society on an annual basis. Nobody, in other words, gets out of this debate unscathed. But, back to the issue. Plenty of white and brown people think black people (good thing we have colors to distinguish us, eh?) have their hands out for entitlements they do not deserve. Every overweight black female with five children reinforces the white racial stereotype, stated in private, that ignorance is a trait of such women. Also, black males are fundamentally lazy, so the argument goes. Attaching a multi-syllabic series of Latin and African names to these children does not disguise the fact that whites in particular will view that name as cause for suspicion. Not all whites, but enough to cause a backlash of stout animosity even in the face of evidence to the opposite. This is odd since plenty of white people are lousy parents and, you may recall, white families mistreat their children at an alarming rate.

*Robertlifer (blog comments); "The people of Baltimore do not want the cops to do their jobs. They want to blame the white man for the laziness and poor upbringing of their black male youths. Tired of hearing this. There are many white boys that have struggled and worked their way out of the ghetto. Blacks want but do not care enough. They only care when one of their own is killed. Just glad they are mostly killing each other. Poor thing to say but, it is what it is..."*

So, is this an issue that resembles a Gordian Knot? Are a disproportionate number of black parents simply not "good enough" as mentors and parents? Before you nod or shake your head, I would like to mention that I was raised in a relatively poor (low middle income) family. I was a devoted delinquent, starting about age 10. My parents, sometimes, would drive me to the nearby orphanage and threaten to leave me at the doorsteps for being such a shitty son. Sometimes my mother would smack me or shout at me in despair. I was not lazy. It was reading, writing, and a fertile imagination that drove me onwards. I ran away from home on several occasions hoping for escape. No luck. I fled that home after high school and swore never to act like my parents. My neighborhood was predominantly white. My neighbors blamed black people (later Indians, then Mexicans) for society's problems but their white children were my friends and many of us were delinquents. It was not "the blacks" these neighbors and merchants had to fear; it was us.

- Why do we continue to wage an unsuccessful war on drugs? It is a thrice recycled approached that clearly has not worked. Are there no others ways to resolve this issue? This is the very best we can do? We can design apps to monitor our every bodily function and waste time and resources to crush game candy but we cannot repair the addicted mind?

- Do we really need so many lawyers? There is, according to the American Bar Association, in 2013, 1,268,011 attorneys which seems like a surplus of people whose professional forte is based on the themes of disputes and conflicts (for a price). Alright, skip that question and try this one – how can the public get an accurate assessment of who is a skilled lawyer?

- Why have we militarized the police in direct con-tradiction to Peel's Principles? Police officers are not supposed to be soldiers or even "well armed" militia. These officers should not be dressed in camouflage with knee pads, stun and flashbang grenades on their superhero utility belts, army helmets, night vision goggles, assault rifles, military vehicles, and enough high-power ammunition to reenact the invasion of Normandy. This is the equivalent of putting a 12-year-old boy alone and in charge of the toy store. It has yet to work out well. Give that arsenal of toys back to the federal government. Rockets are for the 4th of July and armored vehicles are for parades. Police officers rarely have the training, aptitude, or ethical justification to own that lethal stockpile of weapons and devices.

- Attention police: the image of a militarize police jumping out of an armored vehicle does not endear you to your employers (the citizens). It only makes us fearful. Peel was right about police being viewed as an occupying army and you are wrong to think otherwise. Even worse, your enemies will arm themselves in anticipation of a civil war; the police versus everyone who no longer supports you and have nothing to lose. If you are hell-bent on taking us to that chasm, and it appears some of you in law enforcement are, then please accept my friendly advice – change professions before it happens. You are an anachronism that cannot evolve with changing social times.

- Why must we continue to function with the motto of "Just trust us? We know what we are doing." when it comes to supporting the local, state and federal criminal justice systems (adult and juvenile)? Both systems, at all levels, have a dense history of abuse, corruption and institutional deviance. This is clearly a rhetorical question – when and how are the judicial actors going to be held accountable?

- Why do the uber rich and corporations rarely get prosecuted, convicted or incarcerated for gross misconduct such as environmental harm, product fatalities, etc.?

- When do we address the urgent issue of mentally ill citizens who are dangers to themselves and to others? Is it not abundantly clear by now that a relationship exists between unsupervised people suffering from chronic, severe mental disorders and crime? Arming ourselves in anticipation of these people plowing through the living room window with a chain saw seems a bit extreme. They need supervised, institutionalized settings with treatment and care. Does anyone think these individuals actually want to be deranged? "Oh yes, please, I want a life of pain and isolation and mockery."

Many types of crimes are linked directly to the absence of sustainable wages, a need for decent parenting, shitty environments (kids sleeping cars make for lousy students), few educational options, sub-standard housing, little or no health care, racism in all of its ugly forms, poverty, language barriers, self-imposed enclaves of religious bigotry, diet deficiencies (well documented links to cognitive and physical growth), mental illness (lots of it) bullying, the social caste system of capitalism built on tiers of wealth (currently at an historical apex never before seen), the presence of gangs (shortened life spans), a popular culture that encourages violence and sexual deviance, the continued exploitation of women (pause here) – for those of you who think many women are not exploited or do not live in anticipation of being victimized, I need you to do two things quickly: 1. Shut the fuck up. Your ignorance and sexist bias is bleeding out of all of your orifices. 2. Consider this – why do women get socialized on how to avoid being sexually assaulted or victimized? Men do not get that level of indoctrination. Answer? Time's up! It is because men prey on women. That is about as simple as it can be. I refer you to the Uniform Crime Reports (FBI):

https://www.fbi.gov/stats-services/crimestats/

Back to the narrative on the allocation of power. There are obviously other factors to consider but all have been discussed to some extent in the academic research. We cannot predict who will be an offender until the deed is done. Predictions would be swell but some people born into poverty emerge as solid citizens with gifts and real visions for the future. Others, in the same setting, fail often and are lost forever. Meanwhile, the headcount of victims continues uninterrupted. How, exactly, can we make some lasting changes that do more than reinforce the existing power structure?

# Reforms

Just like the awkward questions, I offer twenty equally awkward, brief remedies. Others have expressed some of these solutions far more eloquently than I and deserve the credit for their hard thinking. It is hardly an exclusive list, just a starting point.

1. *Eliminate cash bail for minor crimes* and replace with release on recognizance (ROR), schedules for public transportation, and a call service to remind people to appear.

2. *Upgrade and circulate information about the credentials and ideologies of candidates for judgeships and the office of prosecutors.* Make it available at a website prior to elections. We are entitled to know who these

candidates are and, oh yes, please include a detailed breakdown of their respective donors (with amounts).

3. *Update police academy training curriculum.* The police officer standards and training (POST) is most definitely NOT the best we can do; overhaul this beast with an eye to relevance and the fulfillment of Peel's Principles.

4. *Give all offices of public defenders a working budget* (and resources) equal to that of the prosecutor's office.

5. *Release low-level property and marijuana inmates* out of prisons and jails and place them either under community supervision, job training, or enable some to pay off their sentence.

6. *Education* – stop treating metropolitan school districts as bottomless holes of spending with little to nor tangible return (easily confused with corrections, the concluding point of a shitty education). One start is to design measurable, honest, pragmatic programs with well paid, skilled educators at the helm. I have lots more on this reform. Call me.

7. *Demilitarize the police.* Stop this now. Give that military equipment back to Uncle Sam and focus on your original mission – peace and order and service within your communities / jurisdictions.

8. *Strict liability laws for domestic abusers* are long overdue.

9. *Questionable police practices* e.g. civil forfeiture, hot pursuits, corruption are not going away anytime soon. Fix that. We deserve better.

10. *Treat white collar and cybercrimes as the serious mal-funitions of behavior* that they are; go after these pricks with more resources, better trained investigators, and stiffer penalties upon conviction, for starters. Show the rest of society that the scales of justice are not permanently tilted toward the affluent and entitled. Hey! I thought only the lower class had their hands out for entitlements like health care and welfare?

11. *Make birth control options widely, freely available* to teenagers starting with puberty. That is a proven way to interrupt the bitter cycle of children breeding more children (read=unwanted, maltreated, delin-quent kids). Moreover, and this should irritate loads of people, I advocate the option of *reversible vasecto-mies as a court sentence* for male defendants who are slated to be returned to the community under super-vision. No job prospects, no housing, do we honestly want these men to be able to spawn? This includes white collar and cyber criminals. Once the sentence is completed, reverse the surgery and let the repro-duction begin anew! Babies, babies, everywhere! Oh baby!

12. Mental illness is widespread. Each state needs to change its stance on care for citizens with severe disorders. *Open up more secure psychiatric facilities* and provide treatment. It is that simple (not easy or cheap). Start with helping those who do not know how to ask for help. I have been to many of these

facilities. While not perfect they are a much better alternative to wondering the streets for those in need.

13. *Abolish Three Strikes Laws.* This reform is almost embarrassing to include. Currently twenty-eight states have chronic offender or three strikes laws that enable them to keep imprisoning someone. A third offense, no matter how minor or inadvertent, can activate a third conviction and life sentence. I am unsure which is more offensive; life sentences for a third, minor crime or using a rule of baseball to guide us in our sentencing decisions.

14. *Body cameras* must become standard gear for all employees in law enforcement and corrections. If nothing else, this technology can help protect the employee from frivolous and false charges of misconduct.

15. Crimes by and against the homeless continue. *Alternative, long-term and secure housing e.g. refurbished hotels, for the homeless offer cheaper and more sustainable living arrangements.* The crime rate for that population of citizens should experience a steady decline by adopting this approach nationwide. Hey! Here's a thought. To all of you uber rich folks, why not delay the purchase of your next vacation mansion or sports team and underwrite one of the homeless facilities?

16. Addiction. *Treat addiction as a public health issue and shift resources and technology toward a "cure."* Think

of the lives salvaged, the money saved if we approach drug and alcohol addiction as a treatable condition. Can we not discover a reliable way to block the neuro-cerebral nature of addiction? Modern medicine and the pharmaceutical industries certainly have made billions selling erectile dysfunction pills aka boner champs.

17. *Legalize marijuana in every state.* If not, then I challenge those reluctant states to outlaw alcohol.

18. *Uniform sentencing system for all states.* Similar crimes should receive similar sentences.

19. Juvenile justice. Where to begin? *Try disconnecting the links between decrepit neighborhoods and gangs* as a starting point for reducing crime as well as *limiting the number of delinquents who are placed within the juvenile justice system.*

20. *Gun control is long overdue.* The 2nd Amendment is precisely that – an amendment open to adjustment. There is no such thing as an inalienable right to own guns and use them. I bought a new pickup truck in North Carolina three years ago. The purchase included a $250 voucher for a gun of my choice at a shop in South Carolina. The process of acquiring my new 12 gauge shotgun took about twenty minutes, including background check. It should never be that easy.

# Twelve

## THAT LAST PIECE OF CHEESECAKE

*"Our country is now taking so steady
a course as to show by what road it
will pass to destruction, to wit: by
consolidation of power first, and then
corruption, its necessary consequence."*

THOMAS JEFFERSON

Justice is a relative idea. It changes from decade to decade and moment to moment. Sometimes there comes a point in a society's evolution when it reaches a crossroad of choices and the paths radiate in all directions. Conservative, liberal, middle ground, faith based, corporate ideologies, political agendas, core emotions, groupthink (ever popular and ever present), media manipulation of messages and images (get fit!), cultural values and stereotypes, consumerism, cults, social movements (Hey feminists and Teabaggers, I noticed you folks walked by the issue of female offenders), and maybe rap music...... take your pick. These are powerful forces that push us away from a consensus about what to do with the criminal justice system. Everyone seems to own a fixed point of view on the subject which, you may recall from chapter 1, can run contrary to hard facts and proof. Since we all break the law you would think a bit of introspection might be in order about who is or is not worthy of processing in the courts of justice. In the meantime, do not get caught.

For over 30 years I have watched, studied and been party to some of these changes in criminal justice e.g. becoming a certified dispute mediator. I traveled some of those roads of change. Most were a waste of time (not so with mediation). Most of my travels involved walks through dense forests of myths with narrow paths that true believers never strayed from. Stay on the path, stay with "us" and all will be well. Words like noble, sacred, and righteous are used to bind us to the illusions and myths of justice. In America, those myths are what keep most victims and some defendants from rising up and demanding the keys to the courtrooms. In America, those same illusions are used by white, (Christian) power brokers to keep most of us in line with their interests e.g. centrality of wealth, monopolies, constantly re-electing corrupt or indifferent legislators, and so on. In America the criminal justice system has become an extension of wealth and power within a decidedly oligarchic nation of a few haves, some aspiring want-to-be haves who can afford designer handbags, and everyone else who gets public defenders and the slippery end of the judicial stick. Guess which one you are…

The bandwagon effect is stronger than any narcotic and far more fatal. It says do not challenge, do not question the legitimacy of people and institutions in society. Do not draw attention to yourself. The very bad thing about George Orwell's novel 1984 is its predictions and its accuracy about some things, especially conformity and groupthink, within a culture that is told everyone is special and equal when, in fact, we are not. So it is, in my opinion, with the criminal justice system in America. To those in charge of the means of production (look out Marx!) and the accumulation of cash, barrels and banks of it, we have become expendable units of energy (EUE) in the form of workers and a fractious electorate. We are meant to be manipulated by mass marketing and distracted by the media. There remains a chronic problem between a rational debate and the guy who swears the Civil War was not about slavery, or the woman who thinks abortions are of interest to an omnipotent supernatural being, or the group that rallies to argue for its rights to own and carry guns while limiting the reproductive rights of women:

> *"There is a certain class of race-problem solvers who don't want the patient to get well, because as long as the disease holds out they have not only an easy means of making a living, but also an easy medium through which to make themselves prominent before the public."*
> (Booker T. Washington)

Rewards, therefore, are reserved for the submissive (generally speaking) and the hopelessly ignorant (of which there is an abundance). Most defendants, in short, are probably guilty of something. They accept plea deals because the alternative – trial with a high risk of conviction and harsher sentences – is a logical choice among much of nothing. More prisons, for instance, get built if crime is "up" and more arrests are made. Some of these facilities are run by corporations on the stock exchange whose primary goal is profit and share value. It is abundantly evident that high crime and conviction rates are good for the "business" of criminal justice.

http://thinkprogress.org/justice/2014/09/02/3477866/private-prison-investors-see-profit-in-central-american-migrant-influx/

You can imagine how well that works out for the inmates when it comes to cost cutting measures needed to maintain share values, much like my early experiences with a county jail in Illinois. It means shortcuts and lack of services. It means the upper management gets those sweet, sweet bonuses for squeezing the last nickel from every inmate. But hey! – high fives all around the boardroom! You bastards... The beat of capitalism goes on and it is a thumping loud bass that shakes the windowpanes. Justice is bought and sold as a dispensary doles out medications. So, what have I learned through the years? Let me use the closing pages of this guidebook to take a very short trip through my memory map of observations about the criminal justice system. Here goes:

- *Many jails and prison get their budgets based on head-counts,* not the quality of care and safety, and not surprisingly, the inn at the stable is always full.
- *Prosecutors get re-elected based on conviction rates* which are always high which means sometimes the accused is innocent but gets thrown onto the third rail of justice. Zzzzzt!
- *Courtroom work groups expect guilty pleas.* Anything less is a nuisance.
- *Police often illegally seize our property and cash* under false pretenses and use it to fatten their budgets.
- *Crime labs falsify evidence* and help send the innocent to prison. These labs get money from police departments for submitting favorable (false positive) results from cases.
- *To exonerate someone takes years* and bags of money for the investigation. Even if the evidence conclusively proves innocence, the state is not obligated to release the innocent person.
- *Gangs are virulent cancers that deserve nothing but disintegration and eradication.* I no longer believe the explanations of liberals or conservatives as to why gangs need to be understood. Those reasons, after 40 years of gang growth in America, look like excuses for ganglife. My principal response to gangs is - what

a waste of life. I look at their environments and think – own your circumstances. Get organized and use your political clout. That, however, requires that gangs stop shooting and start talking (which they are too unwilling to do). I measure their behaviors and crimes and see nothing but predictable outcomes. Arrest, prison, release, repeat. I look for one solitary thing, one single good outcome resulting from gangs and come away empty handed. Gangs are inexorably linked to violence, ignorance, and racial cultures that will not stop hurting one another long enough to seek peaceful solutions. If this is a hopeless situation, draconian measures are needed because enough of this awfulness is enough. The only effect of gangs in America is to provide a steady stream of customers for the correctional systems.

- *Lethal products and services sold by corporations rarely result in prosecutions.* Under law, a corporation (per the U.S. Supreme Court) is an artificial entity or person. Sue the company, sure, but prosecute a car company for knowingly (intent) building (act) a car resulting in death (concurrence)? No. That sounds suspiciously like all of the elements of a crime but, wait, how about those share values and bonuses? We have a duty to our shareholders. Profits need to be posted, you understand. How about, moments before someone dies because of tainted food, a defective airbag, dangerous toys, poisonous medicines, etc. you upper-management bonus babies show up in time to whisper something soothing in the ears of the dying child or adult? Explain why capitalism, unregulated and devoid of ethics, is such a worthy system for making the very products that are killing some of us? Hmm…that is a tough sell, right up there with justifying private prisons and child labor to make cheap clothes and computer technology for American consumers. It is all about profit and convenience, which makes sense to a limited degree but that does not make it right.  Or just. Can't you folks postpone immediate gratification for a luxury yacht, the purchase of an island, a trophy wife, buying a sports team or huge patch of acreage, and the acquisition of toys for your entitled children, for even a short while? Use some of that gross profit to help mankind resolve the chronic problems of the criminal justice system. Exactly how much money / profit does one person or company need to be happy? Apparently, that need is a bottomless well from which one can never draw enough water.

*"All amassing of wealth or hoarding of wealth above and beyond one's legitimate needs is theft. There would be no occasion for theft and no thieves if there was wise regulation of wealth and social justice."*

Mahatma Gandhi

- "Give early, often, as much as you want and in secret to elections. That, in effect, was the decision of the Supreme Court in the recent case of: *McCutcheon v. Federal Election Commission*, 2014. *There are no longer any ceilings as to how much a wealthy donor or group may contribute to an election.* That should turn out well for those judicial actors and legislators expecting "strings attached" donations from the elite of capitalism. Oh yes, I almost forgot (bad manners) – "thanks Supreme Court for watching out for the interests of the other 290 million of us who cannot afford or want to donate."

http://www.businessinsider.com/supreme-court-mccutcheon-decision-campaign-contributions-2014-4

- What exactly does a nationwide "stay tough on crime" stance mean at the ground level? It means that *many of the chronic abuses listed above will continue without interruption.* It also means, more significantly, that high rates of arrest, conviction and correctional care (public and private) justify inflated budgets and create jobs. To repeat an earlier observation – *crime is good for business.*

If any of these claims are true, and I firmly believe the facts support them, then the criminal justice system, at all levels is long overdue for systemic, major reforms. It could happen but it is improbable if we must cling to our myths like safety blankets to ward off the nightmares. As this book took shape over the course of several months I dreaded coming to the end point. What was left to say? On what issues would I focus as the stage went dark? I chose those problems that, like unwanted party guests, just won't go away. These are, in my opinion, the major problems that cause crime and fit neatly together like pieces in a puzzle.

Poverty; Do not talk about a rebounded economy. Put away the card tricks of statistics. Millions of once employed citizens are hurting for sustainable wages ($34,000) and benefits. They are every bit as valuable as any CEO or legislator or media mouthpiece. If you ever use the "work harder" myth around me, expect a kick to the nuts; stupidity that stupid needs to be punished. Marginal income employment means no safety nets and even less hope for the next generation (say howdy to college graduates and their one trillion dollar student loan debt).

http://www.cracked.com/article_22718_5-soul-crushing-realities-being-poor.html

Parenting; Toxic families make toxic kids. Some people should never breed and some others need to stop. The world needs fewer delinquents and mistreated children. P.S. large families do not help the crime problem. Gangs thrive, in part, because dad is in prison, mom is illiterate, and neighborhoods cannot babysit their delinquents.

# The Cheesecake Theory of Crime

Wealth; Consumerism and materialism means we crave "sales" and cheap products without much concern as to who made them and under what conditions. Frankly, who gives a brass fart about some nine-year-old working 16-hour-shifts in Calcutta at a sewing machine in order to meet the daily quota for Capri pants that will be tagged with a company brand, loaded aboard a cargo ship and shipped to retail outlets around the United States? Say howdy to globalization. A problem here is that globalization obviously moves much needed jobs out of America and infuses the rich with even greater chunks of loot. And none of that trickles down to the rest of society except through taxes, of which the top 10% pay a lower share than the middle and lower classes. Do the elite think an oligarchic state / country in which they buy and sell legislators and agents of the criminal justice system will not eventually lead to widespread dissent and class warfare? It is easy to imagine the "ripeness" of such conditions needed to create this outcome in a sharply divided nation.

Racism; Everyone I know has a touch of racism. For many bitter, ignorant white people the Civil War is not over (the next one should be a humdinger!). Racism infiltrates the criminal justice system turning citizens against one another. Racial profiling is used to stop, search, arrest minority drivers and seize their cash. No worries. Tainting evidence at a crime lab in order to get minority defendants convicted? No worries, no one will ever suspect. My mother-in-law was a member of the Tlingit people of the Pacific Northwest (Alaska), probably the smallest minority in the United States (about 15,000 members). Because of her pale complexion she could "pass for white" during the decades of racial discrimination including "separate but equal" public facilities, schooling, and social anomie for Native Americans. Of course, with the onset of World War 2, all minorities became equally eligible for the draft (but normally placed in support rather than combat roles). They could die for us in wartime but not sit next to us on the bus in peacetime. My mother-in-law escaped the effects of the white racist culture by virtue of a skin tone.

Power; The one thread that binds all the fabric of this roughshod narrative together is that power determines how justice is defined and applied. Definitions, laws, actors, processes, systems and buildings – all these things are instruments and extension of justice. Justice is fundamental fairness applied evenly to all. It can be measured by how we treat the least powerful member of society. Invariably, justice comes at a cost. It is a juggernaut gaining strength as it accelerates and it flattens those who cannot move out of the way. Bogus arrests merged with falsified lab results leading to a coerced plea bargain for a citizen of little or modest means and a stint in prison is a process we can all live without. The most dismal condition for anyone brought into the judicial process is still an accused indigent, a point that bears repeating while standing before the Statute of Liberty or the Lincoln Memorial. He will positively be crushed by the judicial process. The juggernaut moves on towards the next group of victims and offenders.

Juveniles, for instance, get mistreated and exploited while we stand about and wail about the "injustice" of it all. Consumers become prey to unethical companies and their shady practices (monopolies, defective products). And voters slide into voting booths without a scintilla of useful information about candidates seeking election to key posts in the criminal justice system. We believe in the myth that voting matters when, in fact, it makes no difference except to pacify the electorate into believing that we matter. We do not; we complain about a defective criminal justice system yet re-elect the same incumbent judicial actors. We quarrel about the police but do nothing to demand accountability. What passes for change through voting is the façade of hope and the mythical promise of reform. Honest, significant, and fairly applied changes in criminal justice are rare and costly. They require citizens, not elected individuals, to move the agenda of social justice forward. It will certainly not ever happen, history has demonstrated, because of the involvement of the wealthy and people or groups committed to racial superiority and the prevailing power structures.

Which is to say - having money matters. Having property and health care matters. Having fundamental fairness on display in courtrooms, at traffic stops, and in correctional settings matters most of all. We need to believe in the realities of a fair judicial system and discard the myths. The myths misguide us and they slow us down.

Education; If knowledge equates to power then the very last thing we want in an oligarchy is an engaged, educated citizenry. As Frederick Douglass noted, "Once you learn to read you will forever be free." That is a fair statement but it does not go far enough. The ongoing war on public education is a last ditch stand by those who think science is voodoo, testing will satisfy for learning, and who would prefer that the lower classes STFU and be thankful for any semblance of a free education. Schools have evolved into extended families; two meals a day are provided free for indigent children. Before and after school care is available because some parents work two or three jobs. The profession of teaching, however, is devalued. Thousands of teachers are fleeing various states e.g. Indiana, Texas, New York, Illinois, Kansas, North Carolina, and other ultra-conservative havens of white Christian orthodoxy, or exiting the profession entirely. Awful pay, very long hours, meddling parents, inept administrative policies, and many other factors contribute to this state of affairs. My point is this – the absence of a true education grounded in basic knowledge is a condition known as illiteracy. That condition allows others to victimize and exploit the uneducated, beginning with children and ending with incarcerated adults. Not investing in education in a meaningful manner is a profoundly stupid, biased, and self-defeating response. I cannot help but wonder why the advocates of ignorance do not accept the cause-effect link between a lack of education and crime. Could it be that a more educated electorate would be less likely to tolerate white collar and cybercrimes?

So, what do we stand for when it comes to crime and justice in America? We are myth believers that pass on wonderful, humane ideas to our children. Justice is blind. Everyone is equal under the law. In practice, we are as far from those principles as I am from leaping to the moon. In that gap between what could be and what is within criminal justice awful things happen. Innocent people sit in prisons and jails. Corporations sign cease and desist orders for killing and maiming consumers with their products and services. Crooked prosecutors, judges, jailers, parole officers abscond with the public trust. And so it goes, generation after generation. The U.S. Supreme Court did not even begin to address the rights of accused citizens until the 1960's. You know, the basic stuff like right to an attorney and safety from torture at the hands of police who want to extract a quick confession. Fifty-five years have passed, some reforms were implemented but, overall, we still cling to those myths of justice like lifelines on a sinking ship.

We are rapidly creating an underclass that has no faith in or support for criminal justice. It reminds me of England in the 1800's; rioting, the rise of industrialization (machines before people), the wholesale exploitation of human capital, and the timely arrival of Peel's new police force. The conditions for widespread social upheaval seem to be at hand in America. That may not be a bad thing under the circumstances.

We have created a criminal justice system, generally speaking, that needs a sustained, massive diagnostic overhaul. Rotate the tires, check the fluids and make sure the wipers work. Rebuild some of the engine because the crankcase is busted and old. And the transmission is most definitely shot. Too much is wrong and in need of repair in criminal justice:

- Too many unarmed people shot while fleeing the police.
- Too many wrongful charges, false lab results, and convictions.
- Too much punishment out of whack for minor crimes.
- Too many foster care home placements that hurt children.
- Too many judicial actors that can be bribed.
- Too many legislators that are for sale, passing laws that do not promote social justice.
- Too many religions that endorse the judicial systems to their congregations while fleecing them through the crimes and deviant acts of their clergy.
- Too many corporations and executives and "entrepreneurs" getting rich through legally suspect or criminal methods.
- Skewed sentencing systems.
- A public sense that police are out of control in the use of force.

And last, too many of us keep silent about what is rightfully ours. The criminal justice systems, adult and juvenile, can stand reforms. These systems will emerge more honorable and true to the values and ideas of the U. S. Constitution. The agents of change, however, will not be those who support the myths or necessarily work within these systems. They have no motivations or interests in change. Justice, for most people, is still reduced to calling the police in time of need. That's it and maybe that is enough.

But for others, allow me to remind you that the major reforms of criminal justice are invariably due to the efforts of one person or a very small group of people. There's the opportunity. Use your imagination. How does justice look to you? To my Uncle Phil in his ice cream truck, his myths of humanity (and justice) went unchallenged and untested for a lifetime. His myths were a one-note song sung out of key with reality. To me, a more equitable standard of justice is achievable if we dismiss the myths and remember a key premise of this guidebook –

*"When it comes to judicial reforms the meek go unnoticed and the shy go hungry."*
                                        Book of Bob; Epistle IX

So choose. Abandon those programs and practices that clearly do not work and are costly such as DARE, Scared Straight, Boot Camps, and so many others. Eliminate these overvalued, overpriced social experiments and try something new.

Volunteer to become a dispute mediator. Study the campaign laws of your state. Organize with like-minded individuals to create a public forum on the topic of police reform. Be a whistleblower if you can withstand the fury of scorn that accompanies the act. Stand up and become that squeaky wheel of change. Ideas should be in great supply. I have plenty as do you. There is too much at stake to sit at home and hope someone else will accept the challenge of reform.

Unless, of course, you need a final reminder that government works to serve us and not the other way around. In the meanwhile, could I interest you in another slice of cheesecake?

Looking Elsewhere
Le Quattro Stagioni (The Four Seasons); Antonio Vivaldi

Constitution of the United States

The Power of Myth; Joseph Campbell

"Lovely Day"; Bill Withers